McGRAW-HILL
SCIENCE

Macmillan/McGraw-Hill Edition

Richard Moyer • Lucy Daniel • Jay Hackett
H. Prentice Baptiste • Pamela Stryker • JoAnne Vasquez

NATIONAL
GEOGRAPHIC
SOCIETY

On the Cover:
This colorful frog lives in the jungles of Mexico and Central America.
Like other tree frogs, the red-eye tree frog has long legs for
jumping and climbing. It has sucker pads on its feet to help it hang
on to slippery branches and leaves. Eggs are laid on leaves
over water. When the eggs hatch, the tadpoles fall into the water.
The red-eye tree frog spends most of its life in the trees.

Mc Graw Hill

Macmillan
McGraw-Hill

New York   Farmington

Program Authors

Dr. H. Prentice Baptiste
Professor of Science and Multicultural Education
New Mexico State University
Las Cruces, New Mexico

Dr. Lucy H. Daniel
Teacher, Consultant
Rutherford County Schools, North Carolina

Dr. Jay Hackett
Professor Emeritus of Earth Sciences
University of Northern Colorado

Dr. Richard H. Moyer
Professor of Science Education
University of Michigan-Dearborn

Pamela Stryker, M.Ed.
Elementary Educator and Science Consultant
Eanes Independent School District
Austin, Texas

Dr. JoAnne Vasquez
Elementary Science Education Consultant
Mesa Public Schools, Arizona
NSTA Past President

NATIONAL
GEOGRAPHIC
SOCIETY
Washington, D.C.

The features in this textbook entitled "Who's a Scientist?" "Amazing Stories," and "People in Science," as well as the unit openers, were developed in collaboration with the National Geographic Society's School Publishing Division.

Copyright © 2002 National Geographic Society. All rights reserved.

The name "National Geographic" and the Yellow Border are registered trademarks of the National Geographic Society.

RFB&D
learning through listening

Students with print disabilities may be eligible to obtain an accessible, audio version of the pupil edition of this textbook. Please call Recording for the Blind & Dyslexic at 1-800-221-4792 for complete information.

Macmillan/McGraw-Hill

A Division of The McGraw-Hill Companies

Copyright (c) 2002 / 2004 Virginia impression

Published by Macmillan/McGraw-Hill, of McGraw-Hill Education, a division of The McGraw-Hill Companies, Inc., Two Penn Plaza, New York, New York 10121.
Copyright © 2002 by Macmillan/McGraw-Hill. All rights reserved. No part of this publication may be reproduced or distributed in any form or by any means, or stored in a database or retrieval system, without the prior written consent of The McGraw-Hill Companies, Inc., including, but not limited to, network storage or transmission, or broadcast for distance learning.

Printed in the United States of America

ISBN 0-02-280862-0 / 2

1 2 3 4 5 6 7 8 9 027/043 07 06 05 04 03

Teacher Reviewers

Peoria, IL
Rolling Acres Middle School
Gail Truho

Rockford, IL
Rockford Public Schools
Dr. Sharon Wynstra
Science Coordinator

Newark, NJ
Alexander Street School
Cheryl Simeonidis

Albuquerque, NM
Jackie Costales
Science Coordinator, Montgomery Complex

Poughkeepsie, NY
St. Peter's School
Monica Crolius

Columbus, OH
St. Mary's School
Linda Cotter
Joby Easley

Keizer, OR
Cummings Elementary
Deanna Havel

McMinnville, OR
McMinnville School District
Kristin Ward

Salem, OR
Fruitland Elementary
  Mike Knudson

Four Corners Elementary
  Bethany Ayers
  Sivhong Hanson
  Cheryl Kirkelie
  Julie Wells

Salem-Keizer Public Schools
  Rachael Harms
  Sue Smith,
  Science Specialist

Yoshikai Elementary
  Joyce Davenport

Norristown, PA
St. Teresa of Avila
Fran Fiordimondo

Pittsburgh, PA
Chartiers Valley Intermediate School
Rosemary Hutter

Memphis, TN
Memphis City Schools
Quincy Hathorn
District Science Facilitator

Life Science

Consultants

Dr. Carol Baskin
University of Kentucky
Lexington, KY

Dr. Joe W. Crim
University of Georgia
Athens, GA

Dr. Marie DiBerardino
Allegheny University of
Health Sciences
Philadelphia, PA

Dr. R. E. Duhrkopf
Baylor University
Waco, TX

Dr. Dennis L. Nelson
Montana State University
Bozeman, MT

Dr. Fred Sack
Ohio State University
Columbus, OH

Dr. Martin VanDyke
Denver, CO

Dr. E. Peter Volpe
Mercer University
Macon, GA

Earth Science

Consultants

Dr. Clarke Alexander
Skidaway Institute of
Oceanography
Savannah, GA

Dr. Suellen Cabe
Pembroke State University
Pembroke, NC

Dr. Thomas A. Davies
Texas A & M University
College Station, TX

Dr. Ed Geary
Geological Society of America
Boulder, CO

Dr. David C. Kopaska-Merkel
Geological Survey of Alabama
Tuscaloosa, AL

Physical Science

Consultants

Dr. Bonnie Buratti
Jet Propulsion Lab
Pasadena, CA

Dr. Shawn Carlson
Society of Amateur Scientists
San Diego, CA

Dr. Karen Kwitter
Williams College
Williamstown, MA

Dr. Steven Souza
Williamstown, MA

Dr. Joseph P. Straley
University of Kentucky
Lexington, KY

Dr. Thomas Troland
University of Kentucky
Lexington, KY

Dr. Josephine Davis Wallace
University of North Carolina
Charlotte, NC

Consultant for Primary Grades

Donna Harrell Lubcker
East Texas Baptist University
Marshall, TX

Teacher Panelists

Newark, NJ
First Avenue School
Jorge Alameda
Concetta Cioci
Neva Galasso
Bernadette Kazanjian-reviewer
Toby Marks
Janet Mayer-reviewer
Maria Tutela

Brooklyn, NY
P.S. 31
Janet Mantel
Paige McGlone
Madeline Pappas
Maria Puma-reviewer
P.S. 217
Rosemary Ahern
Charles Brown
Claudia Deeb-reviewer
Wendy Lerner
P.S. 225
Christine Calafiore
Annette Fisher-reviewer

P.S. 250
Melissa Kane
P.S. 277
Erica Cohen
Helena Conti
Anne Marie Corrado
Deborah Scott-DiClemente
Jeanne Fish
Diane Fromhartz
Tricia Hinz
Lisa Iside
Susan Malament
Joyce Menkes-reviewer
Elaine Noto
Jean Pennacchio

Jeffrey Hampton
Mwaka Yavana

Elmont, NY
Covert Avenue School
Arlene Connelly

Mt. Vernon, NY
Holmes School
Jennifer Cavallaro
Lou Ciofi
George DiFiore
Brenda Durante
Jennifer Hawkins-reviewer
Michelle Mazzotta
Catherine Moringiello
Mary Jane Oria-reviewer
Lucille Pierotti
Pia Vicario-reviewer

Ozone Park, NY
St. Elizabeth School
Joanne Cocchiola-reviewer
Helen DiPietra-reviewer
Barbara Kingston
Madeline Visco

St. Albans, NY
Orvia Williams

Plants and Animals PAGE A1

Who's a Scientist? PAGE S1

Homes for Plants and Animals PAGE B1

UNIT C · Earth Science

Changes on Earth PAGE C1

UNIT D

Earth Science

The Sun and Its Family PAGE D1

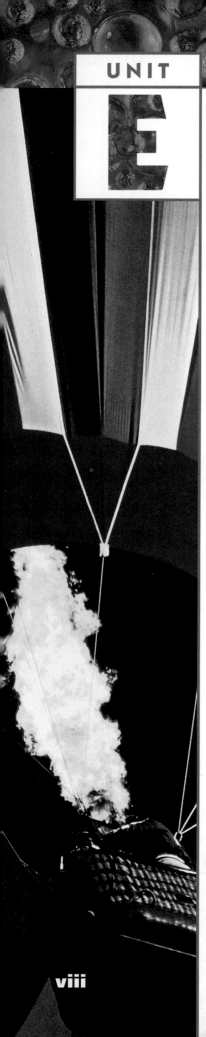

Matter and Energy PAGE E1

UNIT F

Physical Science

Watch It Move PAGE F1

Read these pages. They will help you understand this book.

This is the name of the **lesson.**

Get Ready asks a question to get you started. You can answer the question from the picture.

This **Science Skill** is used in the **Explore Activity.**

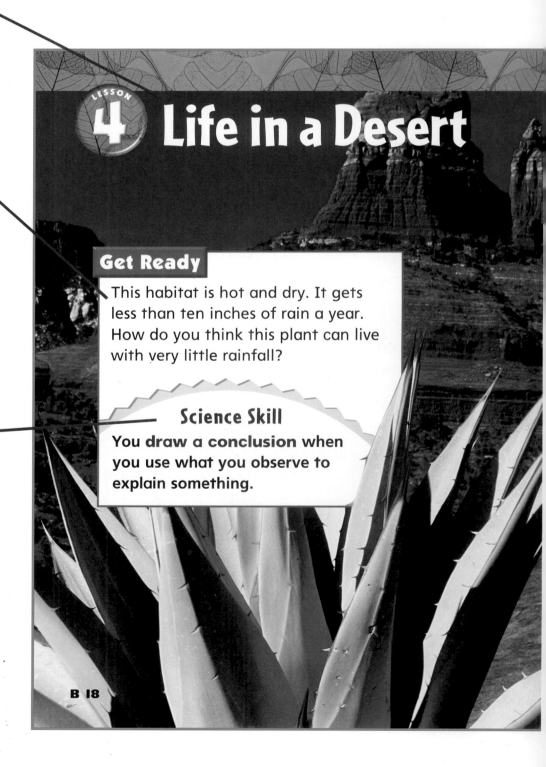

LESSON
4 **Life in a Desert**

Get Ready

This habitat is hot and dry. It gets less than ten inches of rain a year. How do you think this plant can live with very little rainfall?

Science Skill

You draw a **conclusion** when you use what you observe to explain something.

B 18

You can try the **Explore Activity** before you read the lesson.

The **Explore Activity** helps you answer a question.

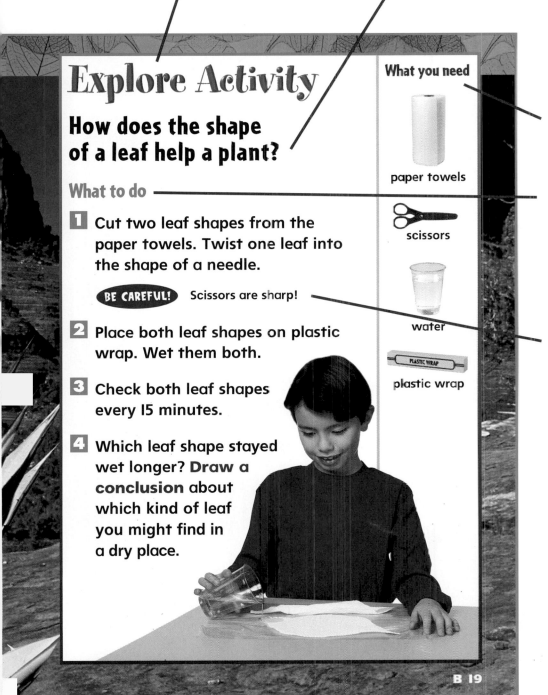

Explore Activity

How does the shape of a leaf help a plant?

What you need

paper towels

scissors

water

plastic wrap

What to do

1 Cut two leaf shapes from the paper towels. Twist one leaf into the shape of a needle.

BE CAREFUL! Scissors are sharp!

2 Place both leaf shapes on plastic wrap. Wet them both.

3 Check both leaf shapes every 15 minutes.

4 Which leaf shape stayed wet longer? **Draw a conclusion** about which kind of leaf you might find in a dry place.

B 19

What you need lists the things you need.

What to do are the steps you follow.

Be careful! reminds you to stay safe.

Reading In SCIENCE

Now you are ready to read.

Before You Read
Read the red question at the top of the page. It will help you find the main idea.

Dark words with yellow around them are new words to learn.

Read
As you read, look for the answer to the red question.

Read to Learn

What lives in a desert?

A **desert** is a dry habitat. It gets less rain in a year than most plants and animals need to live.

Some desert plants, such as a cactus, can live a long time without rain. They store water in their thick stems.

Some desert animals get the water they need from their food.

jackrabbit

cactus

rattlesnake

B 20

This label tells you what the picture is. Pictures and words work together.

lizard

Some deserts are very hot during the day. Many animals hide below ground or under rocks to keep cool. At night they come out to look for food.

▶ How are these living things meeting their needs?

Stop and Think

1. What is a desert?

2. How do some desert animals keep cool when the Sun is hot?

AT THE COMPUTER

Visit **www.mhscience02.com** to learn more about deserts.

B 21

After You Read
This question helps you check what you just read.

These questions check what you learned in the lesson.

Fun activities help you learn more.

Wash your hands after each activity.

Read all steps a few times before you start.

When you see this:

BE CAREFUL!

you should be careful.

Be careful with glass and sharp objects.

Cover your clothes or wear old ones.

Listen to the teacher.

Never taste or smell anything unless your teacher tells you to.

Keep your workplace neat. Clean up after you are done.

Tell the teacher about accidents and spills right away.

Wear goggles when you are told to.

Don't touch plants or animals unless your teacher tells you to.

Tell the teacher about accidents right away.

Listen to the teacher.

Stay with your group.

Never taste or smell anything unless your teacher tells you to.

Never throw your trash on the ground.

Put living things back where you found them.

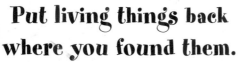

Scientists observe.

Use your senses. Find the word OBSERVE three times in the box below. Did you observe other words? You are a scientist, too!

```
O  B  S  E  R  V  E  G  O
T  O  D  A  Y  E  V  E  N
S  B  H  A  B  I  T  T  O
I  S  O  M  E  R  U  N  S
L  E  D  O  N  E  R  U  N
L  R  M  A  K  E  N  E  W
Y  V  O  B  S  E  R  V  E
S  E  S  C  I  E  N  C  E
```

Scientists measure.

Look at the two flowers.
Which black dot is bigger?
Measure to find out.

Scientists compare and classify things.

Compare the animals in this picture.
Find the animals without legs.
You are a scientist, too!

Scientists make models.

Make a model like this one.
How well did it work?
You are a scientist, too!

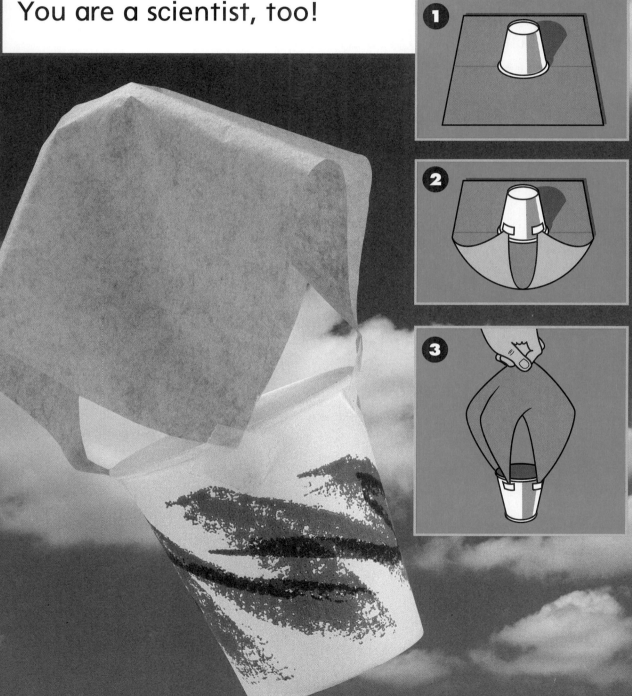

Scientists infer.

Who ate the cookies?
What clues help you know?
You are a scientist, too!

Scientists communicate.

Read each clue below.
Which animal is it?
Tell others your ideas.

1. **This animal is green.**
2. **This animal has a tail.**
3. **This animal has a shell.**

Scientists put things in order.

Name the animals in ABC order.

duck

cow

pig

dog

lamb

horse

Scientists predict.

Predict which of these animals
would be next.

skunk

rabbit

Scientists investigate and draw conclusions.

Investigate to find out which string is not being held. What conclusion did you draw?

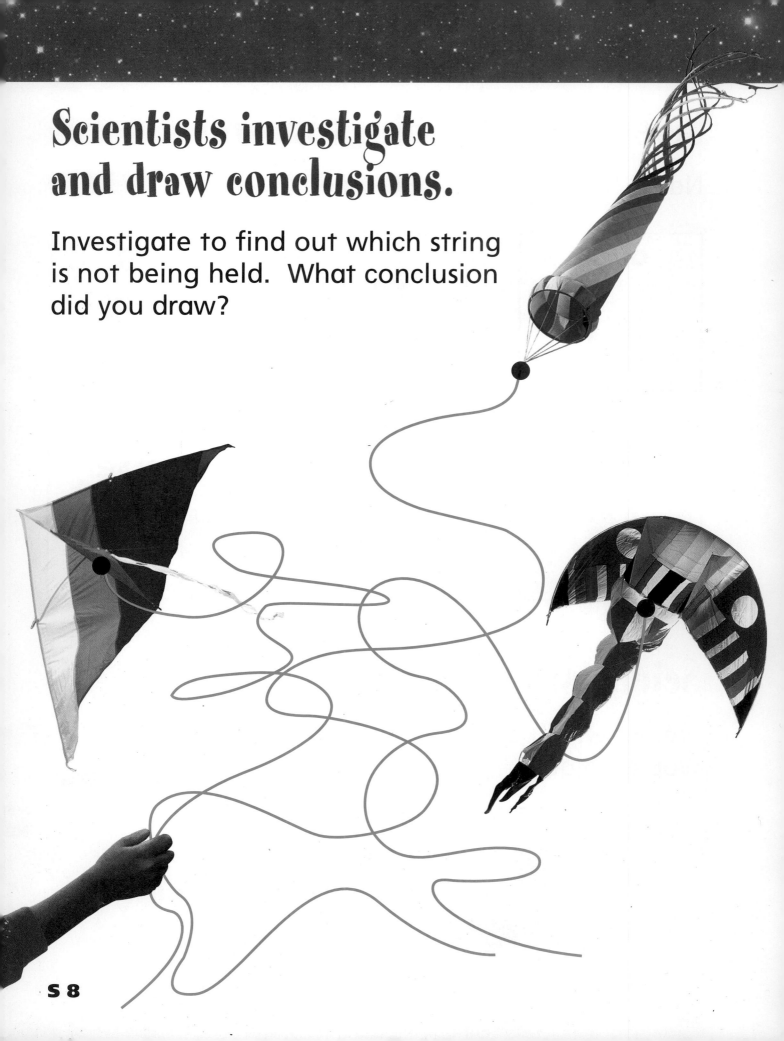

UNIT A

Plants and Animals

LOOK!

Pandas like to eat bamboo, a treelike plant. What else do pandas like to do? Take a good look!

Plants and Animals

Plants

Vocabulary

minerals
flower
fruit
seeds
pollen
life cycle
oxygen

Did You Ever Wonder?

Where do blueberries come from? They grow on bushes found in the wild and on blueberry farms. The best time to pick blueberries is in July. July is also known as National Blueberry Month! Do you know other plants that grow fruit?

Plants Are Living Things

Get Ready

Can you find things in this picture that are living? Can you find things that are not living? Tell how things in this picture are alike and different.

Science Skill

You **classify** when you put things into groups to show how they are alike.

Explore Activity

Which of these are living?

What to do

1 Classify things in your classroom.
List three or more living things.
List three or more nonliving things.

2 Record the lists on a chart
like this one.

Living	Nonliving

3 Share your chart with a
partner. Tell how you knew
how to classify each thing.

Are plants living things?

Like all living things, plants grow and change. To grow, plants need food, water, and air. Like all living things, plants can make other living things like themselves.

▶ **How can you tell these plants are living things?**

tiger lilies

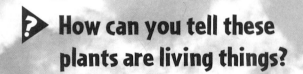

pine tree

How are plants alike?

Plants make their own food. To make food, plants need light, water, and air. They also use **minerals**. Minerals come from tiny bits of rock and soil. They help plants stay healthy.

▶ **How are all of these plants alike?**

How are plants different?

Plants may have different shapes, sizes, and colors. Plants may be as small as a penny or as tall as a house. Many plants have green leaves. Some plants have colorful flowers.

Many plants grow straight up from the ground. Other plants, such as vines, grow up walls or along the ground.

wisteria vine

peach tree

Trees are plants. They have hard trunks. Some trees, such as peach trees, grow fruit that we can eat.

Some plants, such as evergreens, stay green all year. They can grow tall like trees or stay short like shrubs.

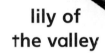

lily of the valley

evergreen shrub

? **How are these plants different from each other?**

Stop and Think

1. How are plants like all living things?

2. How are all plants alike?

3. Name two ways that plants can be different from one another.

AT THE COMPUTER

Visit **www.mhscience02.com** for more information about plants.

Parts of Plants

Get Ready

Why do you think this plant is leaning toward the window? Predict what might happen if the plant was not near a window.

Science Skill

You **predict** when you use what you know to tell what will happen.

Explore Activity

What do leaves need?

What to do

two potted plants

foil

1 Place both plants in a place that has a lot of light.

2 Cover the leaves of Plant B with foil.

3 Make a chart like this one. **Predict** what will happen to each plant. Write it in the chart.

	Plant A	Plant B
Prediction		
Day 1		
Day 2		

4 Record what you observe each day for a week. Keep plants moist.

5 Were your predictions correct? What do leaves need?

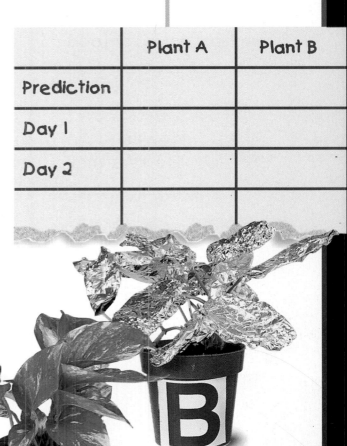

What do plant parts do?

Plant parts help plants get what they need. Some parts help the plant get light, water, air, and minerals. Other plant parts help make new plants.

leaves
Leaves take in air and use light to make food.

flowers
Flowers make seeds.

stem
A stem holds up the plant.

roots
Roots hold the plant in the soil. They take in water and minerals from the soil.

fruit
The **fruit** is the part of a plant that grows around seeds. It protects the seeds.

seeds
Seeds can grow into new plants. Every seed has a tiny new plant inside.

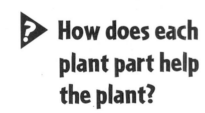

Stop and Think

1. Name the parts of a plant.

2. How do roots help a plant get what it needs?

▶ **How does each plant part help the plant?**

MORE TO READ Read **Plants and Flowers** by Sally Hewitt.

Plants Make New Plants

Get Ready

Think about cutting open a big, orange pumpkin. What do you think you would find inside it? What plant part do you think a pumpkin is?

Science Skill

You **infer** when you use what you know to figure something out.

Explore Activity

Picture
Cards 1–8

Which seeds grow into each plant?

What to do

1 Sort the Picture Cards into two groups. Make one group for grown plants. Make another group for seeds.

2 Observe each group. **Infer** which seeds come from each plant. Match the cards.

3 Tell why you made each match.

Apple Seeds

How do plants make seeds?

Different plants have different ways to make seeds. Many plants grow flowers. Inside a flower is a powder called **pollen**. Pollen can make seeds grow inside a flower.

When an insect lands on a flower, pollen may stick to the insect. Then it carries the pollen from flower to flower.

pepper plant

Pollen makes seeds grow inside the flowers.

flower

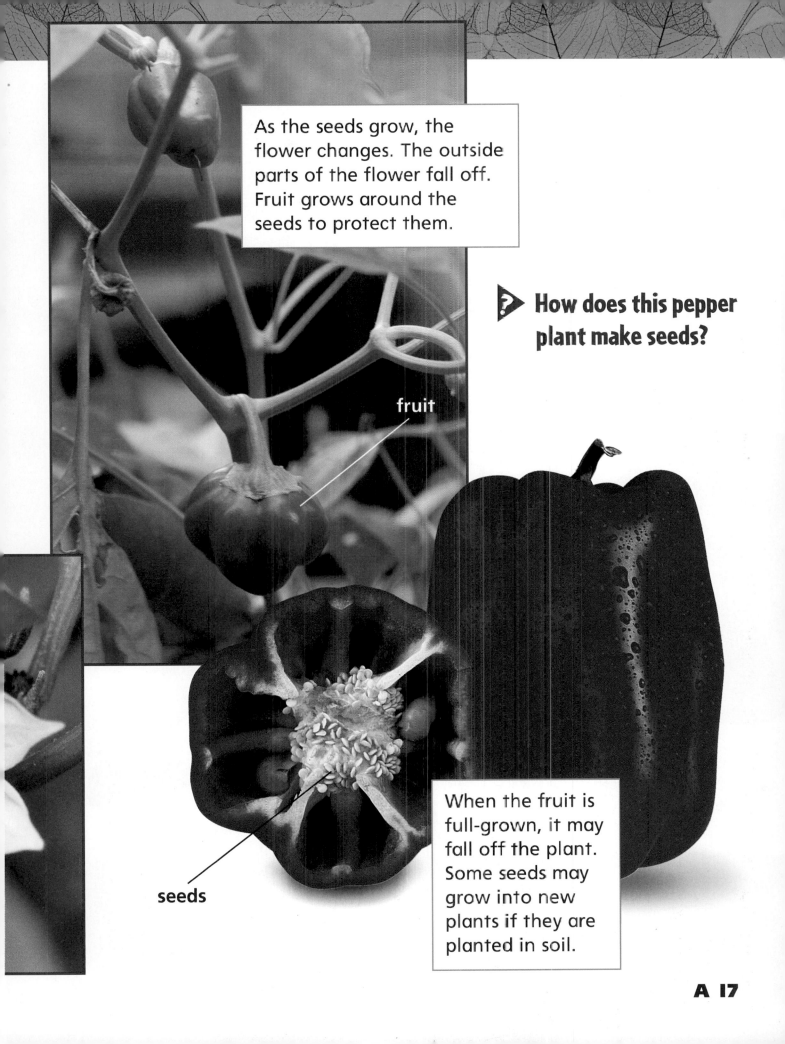

As the seeds grow, the flower changes. The outside parts of the flower fall off. Fruit grows around the seeds to protect them.

How does this pepper plant make seeds?

fruit

seeds

When the fruit is full-grown, it may fall off the plant. Some seeds may grow into new plants if they are planted in soil.

How do seeds grow into new plants?

A **life cycle** shows how a living thing grows, lives, and dies. A plant's life cycle starts with a seed. Inside the seed is a tiny new plant. The outside of the seed is covered by a seed coat. When a seed gets water, warmth, and air, it can begin to grow.

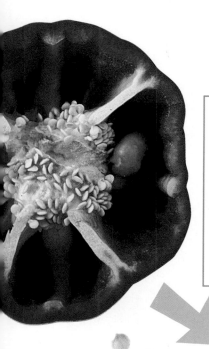

First a small root grows down. The stem grows up. When a stem breaks through the soil, it is called a sprout.

seeds

sprout

seedling

Soon a young plant has leaves and can make its own food. It is now called a seedling.

young adult

adult pepper plant

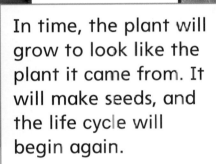

In time, the plant will grow to look like the plant it came from. It will make seeds, and the life cycle will begin again.

▶ **What stages does a seed go through as it grows into a plant?**

Stop and Think

1. What grows around the seed of a plant?

2. How do insects help plants to grow seeds?

3. What is a life cycle?

MORE TO READ   Read **From Seed to Plant** by Gail Gibbons.

Everyone Needs Plants

Get Ready

Have you ever wondered what the world would be like without plants? Look carefully at this picture. What things come from plants?

Science Skill

You **infer** when you use what you know to figure something out.

Explore Activity

What is made from plants?

What to do

1 Go on a plant hunt in your classroom.

2 **Infer** which objects are made from plants. Look for other objects that are not made from plants.

3 Fill in a chart like this one. Show which group each item belongs to.

Made from Plants	Not Made from Plants

How do people use plants?

Many things you use every day come from plants. The cotton plant can be used to make clothes.

Some plants are used to make medicine. One plant used for medicine is aloe. The leaves of the aloe plant contain oil. This oil helps heal minor burns and scrapes.

cotton

aloe

lumber

paper

furniture

pine tree

Trees are used for wood and for paper products. People use wood to build houses, furniture, and many other things.

Most importantly, plants make **oxygen**. People, animals, and plants need oxygen to live. As plants make food for themselves, they give off oxygen into the air.

▶ **What are some ways people use plants?**

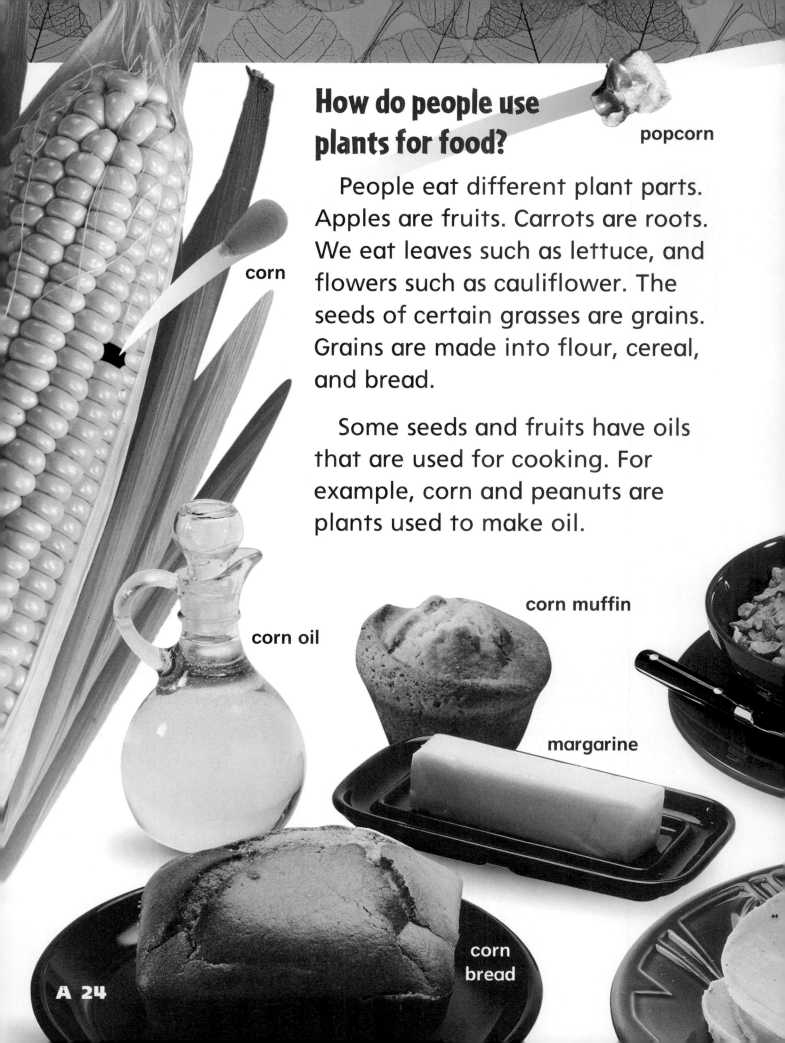

How do people use plants for food?

People eat different plant parts. Apples are fruits. Carrots are roots. We eat leaves such as lettuce, and flowers such as cauliflower. The seeds of certain grasses are grains. Grains are made into flour, cereal, and bread.

Some seeds and fruits have oils that are used for cooking. For example, corn and peanuts are plants used to make oil.

popcorn

corn

corn oil

corn muffin

margarine

corn bread

Herbs and spices are parts of plants used to flavor foods. Some herbs are mint and parsley. Some spices you may use are pepper and cinnamon.

mint

cinnamon

▶ **Where do the foods in these pictures come from?**

cornflakes

Stop and Think

1. What kinds of things do we get from plants?

2. What is the most important thing we get from plants? Tell why.

3. What are some foods we get from plants?

HOME ACTIVITY Look around your home. What do you see that is made from wood or paper?

corn tortillas

Discover State Flowers

Did you know that every state has a state flower? Below is the dogwood flower. It is the state flower of Virginia. What is your state flower?

dogwood flower

Try This!

Learn about your state flower. Go to the library. Look up your state in the encyclopedia. Find out about your state flower. Draw a picture of it.

Plan a Plant Menu

Think about what you ate today. Did you eat any plants or food made from plants?

The Special of the day is Plants.

Try This!

Plan a meal that uses only plants and things that are made from plants. Write a menu and draw what the meal might look like.

Chapter 1 Review

Vocabulary

flower

fruit

life cycle

minerals

oxygen

pollen

seeds

Use each word once for items 1–7.

1 A ____ shows how a living thing grows, lives, and dies.

2 Some plants grow from ____ .

3 Plants give off ____ into the air.

4 Bits of rock and soil that break down are called ____ .

5 The powder made by flowers is called ____ .

6 The plant part that makes seeds is called a ____ .

7 The plant part that grows around a seed and protects it is a ____ .

Science Ideas

8 What do all plants need to stay alive? Write a sentence about it.

9 Which picture does not show
a way that people use plants?

A   B   C   D

Science Skill: Observe

10 What part of this plant is
not showing in the picture?

READ
Juan's Vegetable Garden by Seth Adams
Mr. Hobson's Garden by Marc Gave

Animals

Vocabulary

mammals

reptiles

amphibian

predator

prey

food chain

shelter

larva

pupa

Did You Ever Wonder?

Do animals take care of their young? Some do! A manatee calf will stay with its mother for several years. The mother teaches it where to swim and how to find food. What will this manatee calf look like as an adult?

All Kinds of Animals

Get Ready

There are so many different kinds of animals. Look at these animals. How are they alike? How are they different?

Science Skill

You **classify** when you put things into groups to show how they are alike.

Explore Activity

How can we classify animals?

zebra

tiger

fox

rabbit

fish

snake

What to do

1 Compare the animals in these pictures.

2 Make a diagram like this one. Classify the animals.

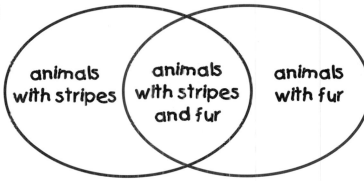

animals with stripes

animals with stripes and fur

animals with fur

3 Write the names of the animals in the correct parts of the circles. Tell how you decided where each animal belongs.

4 Think of more animals that could belong to each group. Write them in your diagram.

What are some animal groups?

Scientists classify animals into groups. To do this, they look at ways an animal is the same as others in a group. Here are six animal groups.

beetle

insects
Insects have three body parts and six legs. They have hard body coverings. Their young hatch from eggs.

rattlesnake

reptiles
Reptiles have dry, scaly skin. Most reptiles lay eggs.

mammals
Female **mammals** make milk for their babies. Mammals have hair or fur. They breathe with body parts called lungs.

lion

amphibians

Almost all **amphibians** begin their lives in water. They often have smooth, moist skin that helps them to live both in water and on land.

tree frog

goldfinch

birds

Birds are the only animals with feathers. Birds have two wings and two legs. They also have beaks and lay eggs.

▶ **How are fish different from the other animal groups?**

butterfly fish

Stop and Think

1. What are six groups of animals?

2. How are mammals and birds different from one another?

fish

Fish live in water. They breathe with body parts called gills. Fish have fins to move through the water.

AT THE COMPUTER Visit **www.mhscience02.com** to learn more about animals.

Animals Meet Their Needs

Get Ready

Look at this fish. What is it doing? Tell how the fish is getting what it needs to live.

Science Skill

You **communicate** when you share your ideas with others.

Explore Activity

What do pets need to live?

What to do

1 Think of a pet you have or would like to have. Draw a picture of it.

2 Imagine you had to leave your pet with a pet-sitter.

3 What does your pet-sitter need to do for your pet? Write sentences or draw pictures to **communicate** what your pet needs.

What do animals need?

Animals need air, water, and food. They also need a safe place to live and have their young.

Different kinds of animals live in different places. Some live on land. Some live in the water. But each animal has ways to get what it needs in the place where it lives.

▶ **What do these birds need to live?**

herons

A 38

How do animals get water and air?

Animals need water. Some drink from lakes and streams. Other animals get water from the food they eat. You need water, too.

Most animals breathe in the air around them. Fish can breathe under the water with gills. Sea mammals have lungs. They must come to the surface of the water for air.

▶ **How do these animals get what they need?**

humpback whale

lions

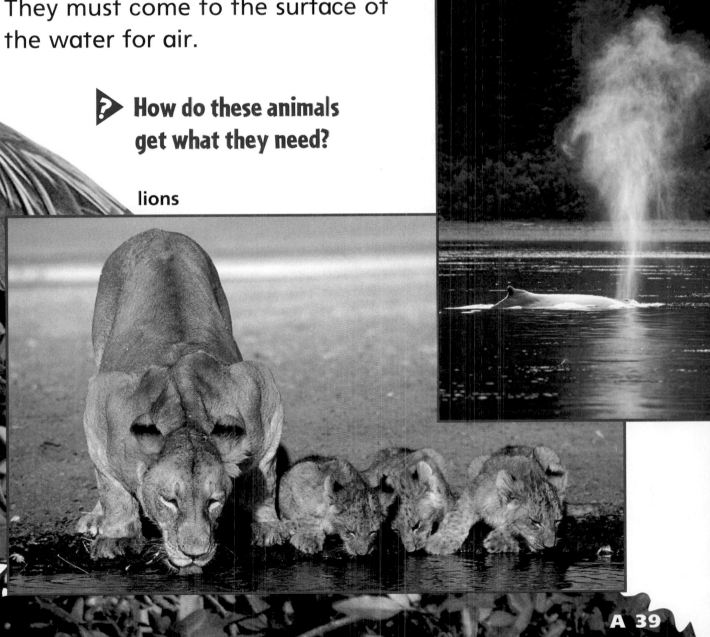

How do animals get food?

Animals use their senses and body parts to get the food they need. Some eat only plants. Some eat only other animals. Some eat both plants and animals.

An animal that hunts another animal for food is called a **predator**. An animal that is being hunted is called **prey**.

Sharks use their senses of smell and hearing to hunt their prey. Their strong tails help them swim fast.

▶ **What do these animals use to get food?**

Raccoons can use their front paws to search for food.

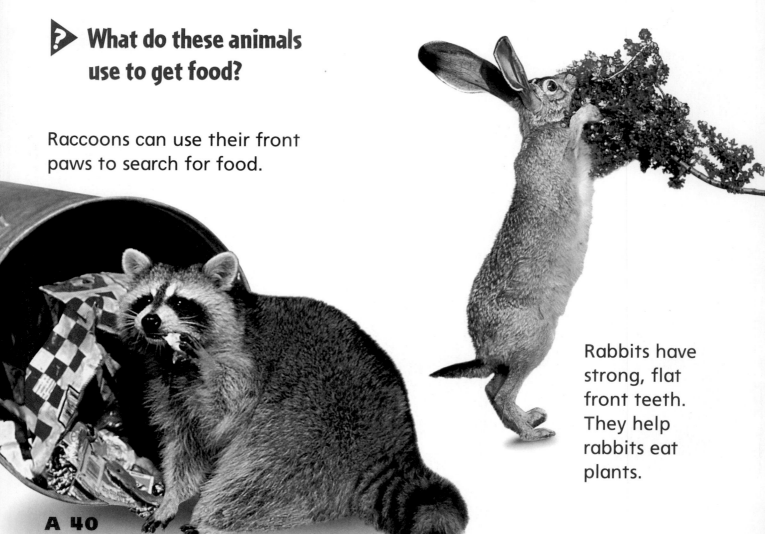

Rabbits have strong, flat front teeth. They help rabbits eat plants.

What is a food chain?

A **food chain** shows how living things need each other for food. Each animal in the chain uses another living thing as food. A cat, bird, caterpillar, and plant make up one food chain.

The leaves use sunlight to make their own food.

A caterpillar eats the green leaves.

A bird eats the caterpillar.

A cat eats the bird.

▶ **How does the bird in this food chain get food?**

How do animals stay safe?

Animals stay safe in many ways. Many use their senses to keep on the alert. Some find **shelter**, or places they can live in and be safe. A mouse can find shelter in a hole. Other animals, like gazelles, can run very fast. Their great speed helps them escape from predators.

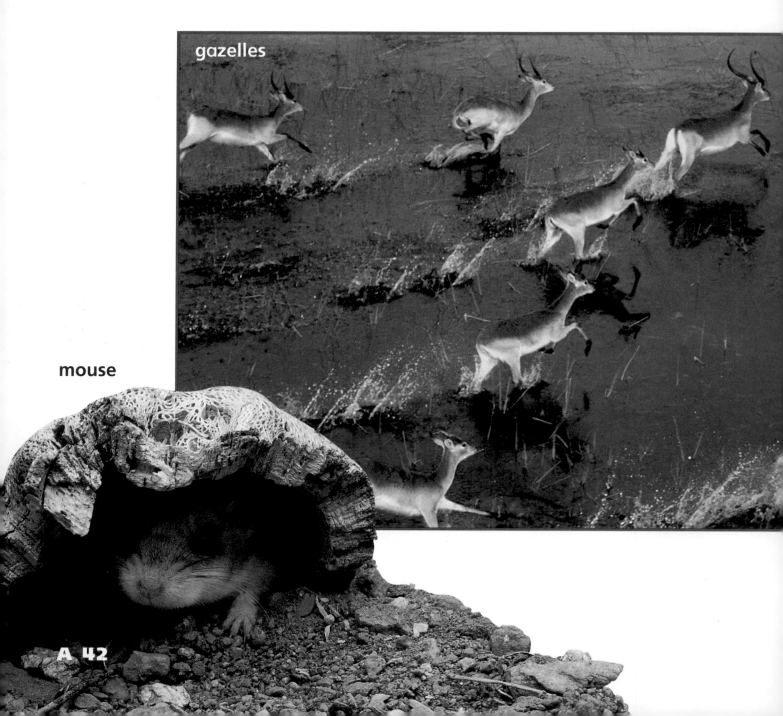

gazelles

mouse

Some animals' bodies help them stay safe. A turtle has a hard shell. When danger is near, it can pull its body inside the shell to keep safe.

This insect blends in with the leaves around it. This helps the insect hide from birds and other predators.

katydid

What are these animals doing to stay safe?

box turtle

Stop and Think

1. What are the needs of animals?

2. What is a food chain?

3. What are two ways that animals stay safe?

 **MORE TO READ** Read **Amazing Animals** by Robin Bernard.

Animals Grow and Change

Get Ready

Look at the young swans. How do you think they will look in one year? Why do you think so?

Science Skill

You put things in **order** when you tell what happens first, second, third and last.

Explore Activity

How do animals grow and change?

What to do

1 Group the Picture Cards for each animal.

2 Put the Picture Cards in **order** to show how each animal grows and changes.

3 Use the cards to tell about what happens first, second, third, and last.

Picture
Cards 9–20

Frog Stage 3

How does a black bear grow and change?

All animals grow and change during their lives. They grow to look like their parents.

eight months old
The cub begins to climb and play. This helps it build muscles. It has most of its teeth, but still needs its parents to find food.

three months old
At birth a black bear cub is blind. It is tiny and has no fur. It grows fast. After three months it weighs about ten pounds. It does not have all of its teeth yet. It gets milk from its mother.

one year old

A cub stays with its mother for about one year. Then, it is nearly full-grown. It can find food on its own. Soon, the young bear leaves its mother.

> **How is a black bear at three months old different from an adult bear?**

adult

An adult black bear can be as long as six feet. It can be two to three feet tall when it stands on all four feet. An adult can weigh as much as 400 pounds.

How does a butterfly grow and change?

Butterflies begin life looking very different from their parents. They go through four stages as they grow into adults.

pupa
The caterpillar forms a hard case around itself. This is the **pupa** stage. Inside the case the pupa changes into a butterfly.

larva
When the egg hatches, a caterpillar crawls out. This is the **larva** stage. The plant is food for the caterpillar. It eats until it is ready for the next stage. Then it attaches itself to a leaf or branch.

egg
A butterfly starts its life as an egg. Most butterflies lay their eggs on plants.

adult

Soon the butterfly comes out of the case. Now the butterfly is an adult. It looks like other adult butterflies of its kind. It waits for its wings to dry. Then it flies away.

> **What happens when the insect is in the pupa stage?**

Stop and Think

1. How does a black bear change during its life?

2. What are the four stages of a butterfly's life cycle?

3. How is a black bear's life cycle different from a butterfly's life cycle?

HOME ACTIVITY Make four pictures, each of which shows a stage of your life.

ALL
ABOUT EGGS

written by
DEBBY SLIER

illustrated by
KA BOTZIS

Eggs-ellent Cards!

Different animals lay their eggs in different places. To find out where, read *All About Eggs* by Debby Slier.

Try This!

Make an egg-shaped card. Pick an animal that lays eggs. Where does that animal lay eggs? Draw a picture of the egg on the front. On the inside, draw what the animal looks like when it is born.

Science Newsroom CD-ROM
Choose **Classifying** to learn how to group things.

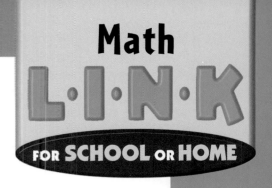

Swim Stars!

Who swims the fastest, a penguin, sea lion, or turtle? Read the graph to find out.

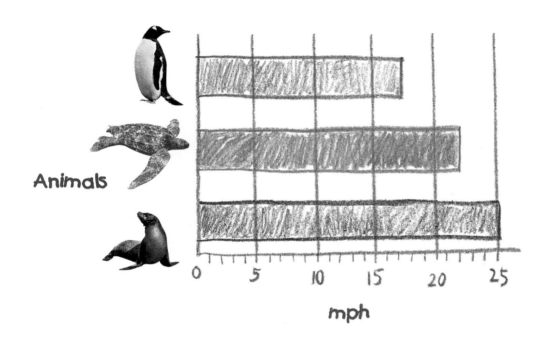

Try This!

1. List the swimmers from fastest to slowest.

2. How many miles per hour can the fastest animal swim?

3. How many miles per hour can the slowest animal swim?

Chapter 2 Review

Vocabulary

amphibian

food chain

larva

mammals

predator

prey

pupa

reptiles

shelter

Use each word once for items 1–9.

1 The Sun, a leaf, a worm, and a bird together are an example of a ____ .

2 An animal that hunts other animals for food is a ____ .

3 An animal that is hunted by another animal is called its ____ .

4 A frog is an ____ .

5 An animal can keep safe in a ____ .

6 All ____ have hair or fur on their bodies.

7 Animals that have dry, scaly skin are called ____ .

8 Another word for a caterpillar is ____ .

9 When a caterpillar makes a hard case, it is called a ____ .

10 Which animal does not belong in this group? Why not?

fox

finch

lion

Science Skill: Put Things in Order

11 Put the life cycle of this butterfly in order.

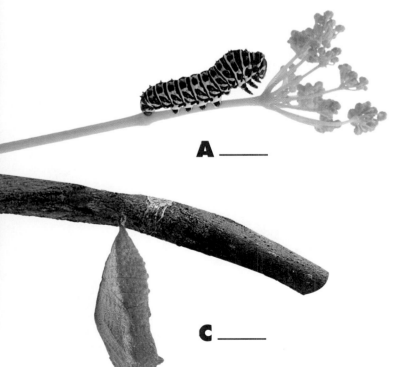

A _____

B _____

C _____

D _____

Monkey Business!

Have you ever needed a helping hand? A place called Helping Hands in Boston, Massachusetts, teaches monkeys to help people with disabilities.

Monkey helpers can turn on lights, open doors, fetch water bottles . . .

First, a monkey stays with a family for about six years. It learns how to be around people.

Next, the monkey stays with a trainer. The monkey learns how to do jobs. Sample jobs are picking up dropped things, dialing a phone, and loading a computer disk. After a year and a half, the monkey is matched with a disabled person.

. . . load a tape into a VCR . . .

. . . and even scratch itches.

What would it be like to have a monkey helper? Write a story about it.

Visit **www.mhscience02.com** to find out more about animal helpers.

A 55

SCIENCE
Workshop

1. Plant Mobile Search through magazines for plant pictures. Cut out at least one of each:

- an object made from plants
- a food made from plants
- a fruit or seed

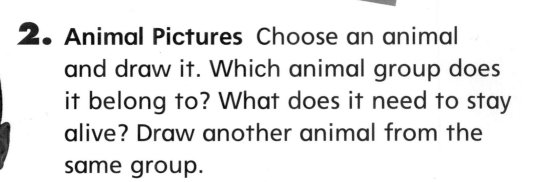

fruit

2. Animal Pictures Choose an animal and draw it. Which animal group does it belong to? What does it need to stay alive? Draw another animal from the same group.

Life Science

UNIT B

Homes for Plants and Animals

NATIONAL GEOGRAPHIC

NATIONAL GEOGRAPHIC

LOOK!

What is this animal?
Where does it live?
Take a good look!

Homes for Plants and Animals

Land Habitats

Vocabulary

habitat
woodland forest
migrate
rain forest
desert
Arctic

Did You Ever Wonder?

Why do prairie dogs pop up out of holes in the ground? They are on the lookout for danger! Their families live below the ground. When a prairie dog sees danger, it barks. What do you think the prairie dogs do next?

Where Plants and Animals Live

Get Ready

Living in the mountains is not easy! The weather is cold. The ground is rocky. Why do you think this mountain goat makes its home there? Talk about what it needs to live.

Science Skill

You **communicate** when you talk, write, or draw to share your ideas.

Explore Activity

Where do animals live?

What to do

What you need

Picture
Cards 21–26

1 Sort the cards. Put the animals in one group. Put the places where the animals live in another group.

2 Match each animal with the place where it lives.

3 **Communicate** why you matched the cards the way you did.

What is a habitat?

A **habitat** is a place where plants and animals can meet their needs. Different plants and animals live in different habitats. Habitats can be on land or in the water. The animals in this picture live near water. This is where they can find what they need to live.

water strider

otter

alligator

The animals in a habitat need plants. They also need each other. Some animals use plants for shelter. Many eat plants. Some animals eat other animals. This bird lives near water because it eats the fish that live there.

▶ **How are these animals meeting their needs?**

Stop and Think

1. What is a habitat?

2. What do animals get from their habitats?

HOME ACTIVITY Take a walk with a family member. Look for plants and animals in a habitat.

kingfisher

catfish

Life in a Woodland Forest

Get Ready

A place with many trees is a good habitat for a chipmunk. What else do you see? How could you show where a chipmunk lives?

Science Skill

You **make a model** when you make something to show a place or a thing.

Explore Activity

What is a forest like?

What to do

1 **Make a model** of a forest. Place a layer of soil and rocks in a large, empty bottle.

2 Place the plant in the soil. Water the soil, and place the pill bug in the bottle. Wash your hands.

3 Cover the bottle with plastic wrap. Poke holes in it. Place it near a window.

4 What does your model tell you about a forest?

What you need

bottle

soil

plant

PLASTIC WRAP

plastic wrap

rocks

plastic spoon

pill bug

What lives in a woodland forest?

A **woodland forest** is a habitat that gets enough rain and sunlight for trees to grow well. Animals may use the trees for food and shelter. Some may make their homes in trees. They eat nuts and insects found there.

raccoon

insects

mushrooms

Animals also use other things in a woodland forest habitat. A fallen tree can be a home for many living things. Plants may grow on the outside of the tree. Small animals may make their homes inside the tree.

▶ **What are some plants and animals that live in this woodland forest?**

woodpecker

foxes

How does a woodland forest change?

A woodland forest has four seasons. In spring many forest animals have their young. Leaves begin to grow on trees.

spring

deer

In summer woodland forests are warm. Leaves on the trees are green. Animals can find a lot of food to eat.

deer mouse

summer

In fall the weather gets cool. The leaves on many trees change color and fall to the ground. Sometimes plant seeds stick to animals. Animals move them to new places where they may grow.

fall

bison

Some forest animals store food for the winter. Many birds **migrate**, or move to warmer places.

chipmunk

In winter many trees have no leaves. It is cold and food is harder to find. Some animals go into a deep sleep.

▷ **How do the trees in a woodland forest change during the four seasons?**

Stop and Think

1. What is a woodland forest?
2. How do animals help the plants of a woodland forest?
3. What do some animals do in the fall?

HOME ACTIVITY

Make a book of seasons. Draw a picture of what you do in each season.

winter

Life in a Rain Forest

Get Ready

These fuzzy creatures are leaf bats. They live in a habitat called a rain forest. How are they using the leaf to meet their needs?

Science Skill

You **infer** when you use what you know to figure something out.

Explore Activity

How can a rain forest animal find shelter?

paper plate

cotton balls

glue

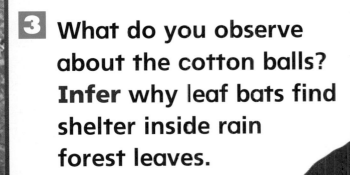
aluminum tray

water

What to do

1 Fold a paper plate in half. Glue six cotton balls inside the fold.

2 Stand up the plate like a tent. Put it in the tray. Pour a little water over the paper plate.

3 What do you observe about the cotton balls? **Infer** why leaf bats find shelter inside rain forest leaves.

What lives in a rain forest?

A **rain forest** is a habitat where it rains almost every day. It is warm in many rain forests. There can be more than 70 inches of rain each year. Because there is a lot of rain, many trees and plants grow well. The trees and plants are food and shelter for many animals.

A tree frog finds water.

An ocelot hunts for food.

There are many tall trees in a rain forest. The tops of the trees get a lot of sunlight. Not as much sunlight reaches the rain forest ground.

Monkeys and parrots are two kinds of animals that live in the tops of trees. They eat the leaves, fruits, and nuts that grow there.

parrot

monkey

> **How do these rain forest animals get what they need?**

Stop and Think

1. Describe a rain forest.
2. How do some rain forest animals use plants?

MORE TO READ

Read **Nature's Green Umbrella: Tropical Rain Forests** by Gail Gibbons.

Life in a Desert

Get Ready

This habitat is hot and dry. It gets less than ten inches of rain a year. How do you think this plant can live with very little rainfall?

Science Skill

You **draw a conclusion** when you use what you observe to explain something.

Explore Activity

How does the shape of a leaf help a plant?

What you need

paper towels

scissors

water

plastic wrap

What to do

1 Cut two leaf shapes from the paper towels. Twist one leaf into the shape of a needle.

BE CAREFUL! Scissors are sharp!

2 Place both leaf shapes on plastic wrap. Wet them both.

3 Check both leaf shapes every 15 minutes.

4 Which leaf shape stayed wet longer? **Draw a conclusion** about which kind of leaf you might find in a dry place.

What lives in a desert?

A **desert** is a dry habitat. It gets less rain in a year than most plants and animals need to live.

Some desert plants, such as a cactus, can live a long time without rain. They store water in their thick stems.

Some desert animals get the water they need from their food.

jackrabbit

cactus

rattlesnake

lizard

Some deserts are very hot during the day. Many animals hide below ground or under rocks to keep cool. At night they come out to look for food.

▶ **How are these living things meeting their needs?**

Stop and Think

1. What is a desert?

2. How do some desert animals keep cool when the Sun is hot?

AT THE COMPUTER

Visit **www.mhscience02.com** to learn more about deserts.

Life in the Arctic

Arctic fox in summer

Get Ready

This Arctic fox had a dark coat last summer. Then its coat turned white in winter. What color coat do you think the fox will have next summer? Tell why.

Science Skill

You **predict** when you use what you know to tell what you think will happen.

Arctic fox in winter

Explore Activity

white paper

20 white circles

20 brown circles

How can color help animals hide?

What to do

1 Fold the white paper. Spread out the circles on the inside fold. Cover the circles.

2 **Predict** which color circles will be easier to see and pick up.

3 Your partner will uncover the circles for ten seconds. One at a time, pick up as many circles as you can.

4 How many circles of each color did you pick up? Record these numbers. How does color make it easier or harder to pick up the circles?

What lives in the Arctic?

The **Arctic** is a very cold place near the North Pole. Snow is on the ground for much of the year. It melts for only a short time in the summer.

In summer plants can grow. They grow very low to the ground. This helps them stay safe from strong winds. Many animals eat these plants.

Arctic plants

musk ox

caribou

Arctic terns

In winter most plants die. Animals that eat plants migrate, or move, to warmer places to find food.

Some animals have white winter coats to blend in with the snow. This helps keep them safe from predators. Polar bears make snow dens. Safe in the dens, the female bears can give birth to their cubs.

▷ **How are these living things meeting their needs?**

polar bears

Stop and Think

1. When do most plants grow in the Arctic?

2. Why do some animals leave the Arctic in the winter?

MORE TO READ

Read **Crinkleroot's Guide to Knowing Animal Habitats** by Jim Arnosky.

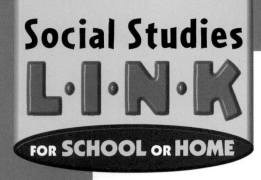

What is your habitat like?

You have learned about different kinds of habitats. Observe the plants and animals that live near you. You live in a habitat, too.

Try This!

Look at these pictures. Compare the habitat where you live with one of these habitats. Write about it.

Make a Rainfall Graph

You have learned that different habitats get different amounts of rainfall. Each year a desert gets less than 10 inches of rain. A rain forest can get more than 72 inches of rain.

Try This!

Make a bar graph that shows the amount of rain that falls in a desert and in a rain forest.

Vocabulary

Arctic

desert

habitat

migrate

rain forest

woodland forest

Use each word once for items 1–6.

1 A place where plants and animals find what they need to live is a ____ .

2 A habitat where very little rain falls is called a ____ .

3 To travel from one habitat to another is to ____ .

4 A habitat where many trees grow and seasons change is called a ____ .

5 A habitat that gets rain almost every day is a ____ .

6 Snow is on the ground for much of the year in the ____.

Science Ideas

7 Which bar on the graph shows how much water a desert gets in a year?

Rain forest								
Desert								

0   10   20   30   40   50   60   70   80

inches of rain

8 Which of these animals does not live in a desert? Where does it live? How do you know?

rattlesnake

chipmunk

lizard

Science Skill: Communicate

9 How does the color of this animal help it stay safe in the Arctic winter? Write about it.

READ
A Science Project for George
by Jennifer Jacobson

Water Habitats

Vocabulary

pond

stream

ocean

food web

pollution

recycle

Did You Ever Wonder?

How do some ocean animals eat their food? A sea otter floats on its back with a flat stone on its chest. Then it uses the stone to open shellfish! What else might you find in an ocean habitat?

Life in a Fresh Water Habitat

Get Ready

Quack! This duck family lives in a pond. They spend much of their day in the water. How do you think ducks are able to stay dry?

Science Skill

You **infer** when you use what you know to figure something out.

Explore Activity

How does a duck stay dry?

paper

scissors

crayons

cup of water

spoon

What to do

1 Trace two ducks on paper.
Cut them out.

BE CAREFUL! Scissors are sharp!

2 Use a crayon to color both sides of
one duck. Press hard. Make sure no
white space is left on the paper.
Do not color the second duck.

3 Drip water on one side
of each paper duck.
Use a spoon. Which
one stayed drier? Why?

4 Infer how a duck's
feathers help it
stay dry.

cattails

What lives in a pond?

A **pond** is a fresh water habitat. Fresh water has little or no salt in it. Like water in a pool, pond water stays in one place. Plants grow in and around the pond. Some plants even float on the water.

bullfrog on water lily

Many pond fish eat water plants and insects. Birds make nests with pond grass. Beavers build homes with branches from nearby trees.

beaver

A pond can change through the year. Some ponds freeze in the winter. Fish swim below the ice. Turtles and frogs dig into the mud for warmth. Some insects sleep in the soil near the pond.

mosquito

perch swimming under ice

In summer a pond may dry up if there is not enough rain. Some pond animals must find new homes.

▷ **How do these animals get what they need in a pond habitat?**

loon

What lives in a stream?

A **stream** is a fresh water habitat with moving water. Salmon swim in streams. Sometimes they swim against the flow of the water to find a place to lay eggs.

salmon

otter

Otters find shelter on the sides of streams. Many insects buzz above the stream.

Some animals, such as otters and birds, dive in the water to find food to eat.

gray wagtail

dragonfly

▶ **How are these animals meeting their needs?**

Stop and Think

1. How are ponds and streams alike? How are they different?

2. What do some pond animals do in the winter?

3. What are some ways animals find food in fresh water habitats?

AT THE COMPUTER Visit **www.mhscience02.com** to learn more about fresh water habitats.

Life in a Salt Water Habitat

Get Ready

Many animals live in the ocean and near the beach. What kind of habitat do these two animals live in?

Science Skill

You **observe** when you use your senses to learn about the world around you.

Explore Activity

What lives in a salt water habitat?

What to do

1 Fill each container with two cups of water. Add two teaspoons of salt to one container. Mix it.

2 Add $\frac{1}{4}$ teaspoon of brine shrimp eggs to the fresh water. Add the same amount to the salt water.

3 Check each container every day. **Observe** what happens. Use a hand lens.

4 Can brine shrimp grow in both containers? Tell why or why not.

What you need

brine shrimp eggs

2 clear containers

spoon

salt

measuring spoon

measuring cup

hand lens

What lives in the ocean?

An **ocean** is a large, deep body of salt water. Oceans cover three-fourths of Earth. The salty water can be up to seven miles deep! It is deeper in some places than it is in others.

Most ocean animals and plants need salt water to live. They cannot live in fresh water.

dolphin

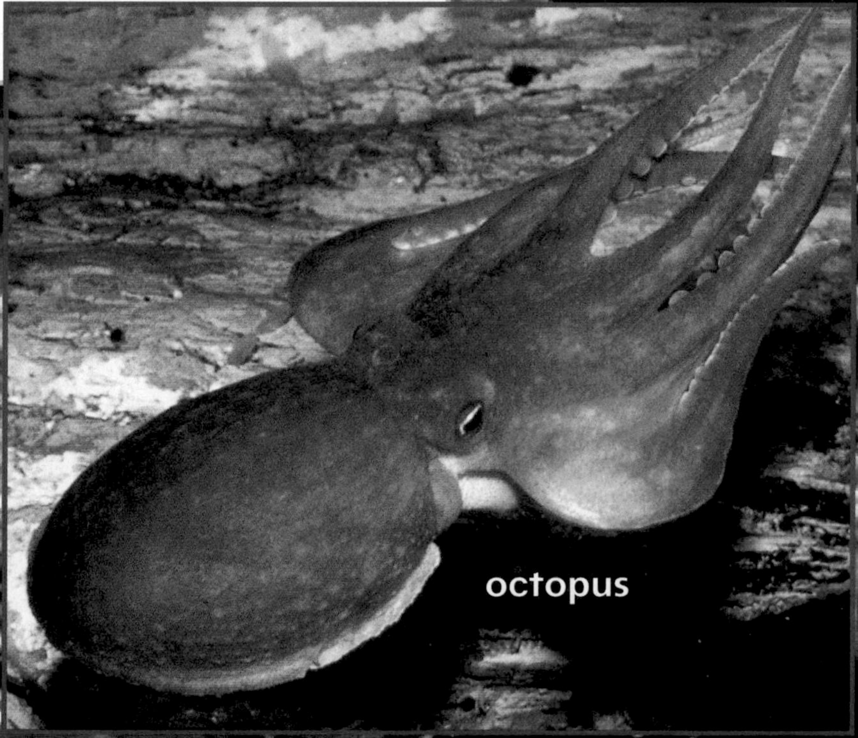

octopus

coral with tropical fish

B 40

Many fish search for sea plants or other fish to eat. Dolphins and whales also swim to find food. They are mammals, so they must come to the surface to breathe air.

starfish

Different plants and animals live in different parts of the ocean. Some animals live near the shore.

▷ **How are all of these animals alike?**

eel

lobster

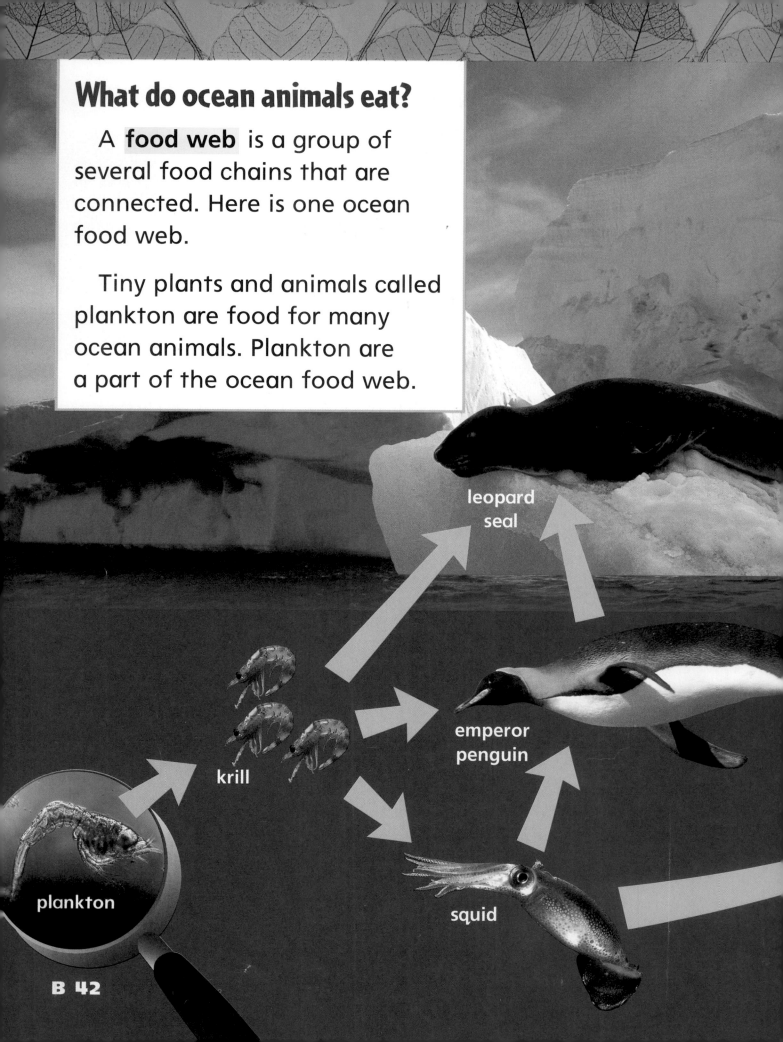

What do ocean animals eat?

A **food web** is a group of several food chains that are connected. Here is one ocean food web.

Tiny plants and animals called plankton are food for many ocean animals. Plankton are a part of the ocean food web.

leopard
seal

emperor
penguin

krill

plankton

squid

Many fish and krill eat plankton. Larger fish, seals, and penguins eat these fish. Some whales then eat seals and penguins. The arrows in this picture show what is food for each animal.

▶ **What is happening in this food web?**

Stop and Think

1. What is an ocean?

2. How deep can an ocean get in some places?

3. What is a food web?

MORE TO READ Read **The Magic School Bus on the Ocean Floor** by Joanna Cole.

killer whale

Caring for Earth's Habitats

Get Ready

What if the ocean were covered with black slime? That is what happens when oil spills into the water. What do you think this oil spill will do to the bird and its habitat?

Science Skill

You **predict** when you use what you know to tell what you think will happen.

Explore Activity

What can oil do to a bird's feathers?

What to do

1 Put the feather in the water. **Predict** what will happen if you pour oil into the water.

2 Pour oil into the water.

3 Tell what happens to the feather.

4 Try to remove the oil from the feather and the water. Use paper towels. Is it easy or difficult to do? Wash your hands when done.

tray of water

feather

cup of oil

paper towels

How can we care for the water?

We can care for the water by making less **pollution**. Pollution is garbage that harms land, water, or air. It hurts both living and nonliving things. There are now laws against pollution.

But laws are not enough. We can help keep water clean by picking up trash. We can tell others about the dangers of dumping waste in water.

▷ **How are these people caring for a water habitat?**

oil spill

Workers help clean up a bird after an oil spill.

How can we care for the air?

Cars and factories can cause air pollution. People are working to make the air cleaner. We can help keep the air clean by riding bikes and walking.

▷ **How are these people caring for air?**

air pollution

How can we care for the land?

Every day trees are cut down to clear land for building. Many trees are also cut down for wood and paper. We can help care for the land by planting trees. Tree leaves give off oxygen for us to breathe. Tree roots keep soil from blowing or washing away. Planting trees also makes homes for animals.

cleared land

planting trees

We throw away tons of garbage every year. Much of this garbage goes to big pits in the ground called landfills. Landfills are getting too crowded to fit more garbage.

landfill

We can cut down on waste. We can **recycle** paper, glass, cans, and plastic. Recycled waste can be made into new things and used again.

▷ **How are these people caring for the land?**

Stop and Think

1. What is pollution?

2. What can you do to clean up the water, land, and air?

3. How does recycling help the garbage problem?

HOME ACTIVITY What can you do to cut down on trash at home?

recycling

Go Fishing for Facts

Fish come in all shapes and sizes. They live all over the world. Find out about some interesting ocean fish. Read *Fishy Facts* by Anne Miranda.

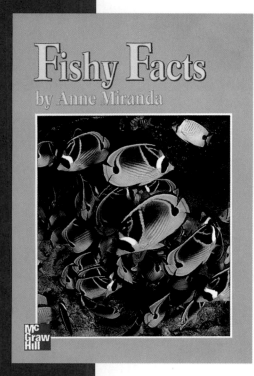

Fishy Facts
by Anne Miranda

McGraw Hill

Try This!

Use your library to find out more about fish. Pick one fish that you find interesting. Draw it on one side of a piece of paper. Write your own fishy facts on the other side.

Science Newsroom CD-ROM Choose **Don't Be Dinner** to learn how animals hide.

Recycled Art

Do you think art can be made by only drawing or painting? Think again! Some artists use materials that would be trash.

Try This!

Gather things you no longer need. Think of a sculpture you want to make. Glue the pieces together to create your own recycled art!

Chapter 4 Review

Vocabulary

food web

ocean

pollution

pond

stream

recycle

Use each word once for items 1–6.

1 Several food chains together make up a ____ .

2 Waste that harms the land, water, and air is called ____ .

3 A fresh water habitat that flows is called a ____ .

4 When you save cans so they can be made into new things, you ____ .

5 A fresh water habitat that stays in one place is called a ____ .

6 A large body of salt water is called an ____ .

Science Ideas

7 What do pond turtles do for warmth during winter?

8 What do beavers use to make their homes?

9 How are a pond and an ocean different?

Science Skill: Classify

10 Do these plants and animals live in fresh water or salt water? List them in two groups.

crab

frog

lily pad

killer whale

READ
River Home by Susan Blackaby

Mark Plotkin

Botanist

As a child, Mark Plotkin loved to explore the swamps near his Louisiana home. He studied the different kinds of plants that grew there. Today, Mark studies plants in the Amazon rain forest in South America. He learns about ways that people use plants.

Mark has learned how some rain forest plants cure sick people. But now rain forests are in danger. Many trees and other plants are cut down or burned. So Mark works to help save rain forests.

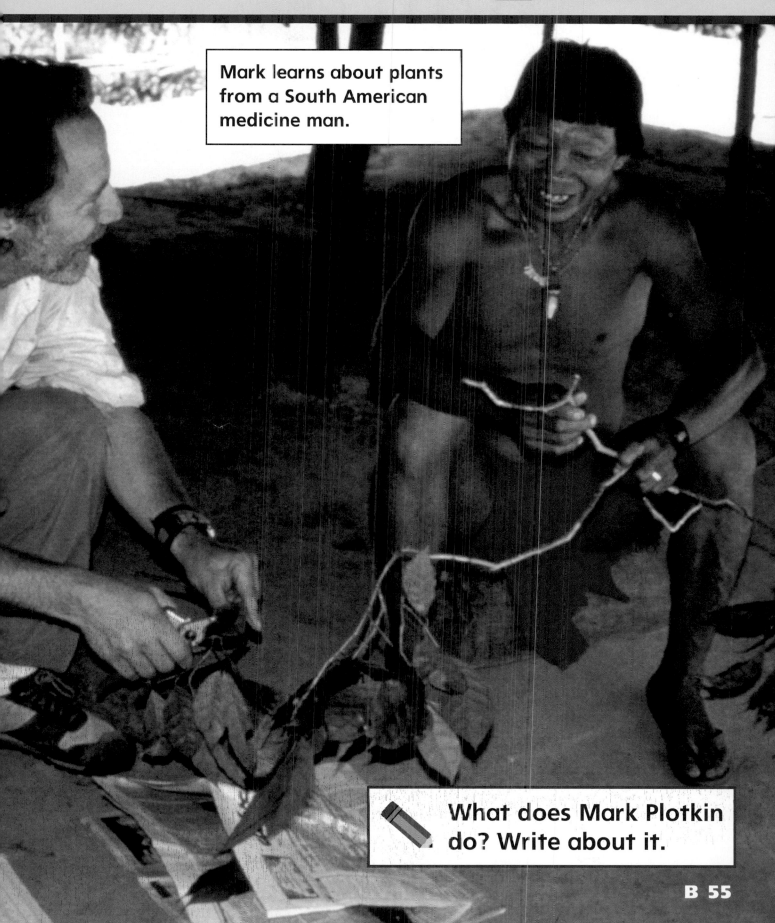

Mark learns about plants from a South American medicine man.

What does Mark Plotkin do? Write about it.

SCIENCE
Workshop

1. **Habitat Story** Choose a plant or animal that lives in a land habitat that you just read about. Write a short story about your plant or animal. What does it need to live in its habitat? How does it get what it needs?

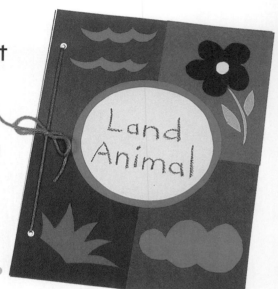

2. **Water Animal Skit** Think of an animal that lives in a water habitat. Pretend you are that animal and act out a story.

Earth Science

UNIT C
Changes on Earth

NATIONAL GEOGRAPHIC

LOOK!

What is happening in this picture? Where do you think the water is coming from? Take a good look.

Changes on Earth

Vocabulary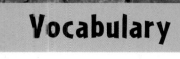

evaporate

water vapor

condense

water cycle

precipitation

erosion

earthquake

landslide

volcano

Did You Ever Wonder?

How fast are tornado winds? Tornado wind speeds are often faster than 300 miles per hour! That's more than twice as fast as most race cars go. Have you ever seen bad weather?

C 3

1 Water and Our Weather

Get Ready

Have you ever been caught in the rain?
Did you know it was going to rain?
Could you tell by looking at the sky?

Science Skill

You **draw a conclusion** when you use what you observe to explain what happens.

Explore Activity

Where does water for rain come from?

goggles

cup

sand

cup of water

plastic bag

What to do

1 Put sand into an empty cup. Add water until the sand is damp.

> **BE CAREFUL!** Wear goggles.

2 Put the cup into a plastic bag. Seal it. Put the bag in a sunny place.

3 After a few hours, observe the bag. What do you see?

4 Draw a conclusion about what happened.

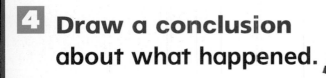

How can water change?

Heat can change water. Heat causes water to **evaporate**, or change into gas. When water evaporates, it goes into the air. Water that goes into the air is called **water vapor**. You can not see water vapor.

Water vapor can be changed back into liquid. Cool air makes water vapor **condense**, or change into a liquid. On a cool morning, you may see tiny drops of water, called dew, on the grass. This is condensed water vapor.

Water condenses on a spider web.

▷ **What happens to the water from the boy's sweatshirt?**

What is the water cycle?

The water on Earth is always changing. It changes from ice to liquid to water vapor and back again. Water moves between the ground and the sky over and over. This movement of water is called the **water cycle**.

1 Heat from the Sun evaporates water.

2 Water vapor rises. Then it cools and condenses into tiny drops of water.

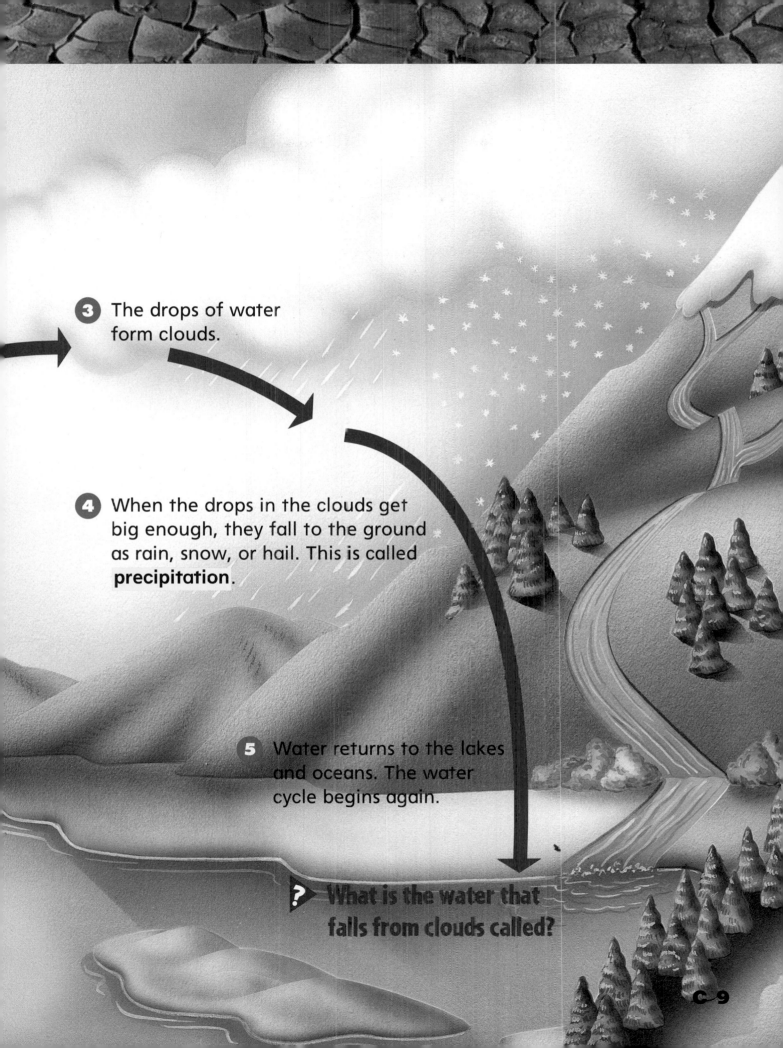

3 The drops of water form clouds.

4 When the drops in the clouds get big enough, they fall to the ground as rain, snow, or hail. This is called **precipitation**.

5 Water returns to the lakes and oceans. The water cycle begins again.

? What is the water that falls from clouds called?

What are some special kinds of weather?

Some weather can cause big changes on Earth. We can be warned ahead of time when storms are coming.

A hurricane is a very large storm. It can cause floods and harm beaches.

A tornado is a storm with very fast winds moving in a cone shape. The winds can cause lots of destruction.

hurricane

tornado

drought

flood

If a lot of rain falls quickly, the ground can not soak up all the water. Too much water can make a river overflow. These things can cause floods.

When a place does not get rain for a long time, it is called a drought. The land dries up. Plants and animals can not get the water they need.

▶ How can weather change Earth?

Stop and Think

1. What happens to water when it evaporates?

2. What is the water cycle?

3. What causes a flood?

AT THE COMPUTER Visit **www.mhscience02.com** to learn more about weather.

Earth Can Change Slowly

Get Ready

Have you ever seen rocks like this? Rocks are very hard. Do you think you could change the shape of a rock? Tell how.

Science Skill

You **communicate** when you share what you know.

Explore Activity

How can you change rocks?

rocks

What to do

1 Look at the rocks with a hand lens. Rub them on sandpaper. **Communicate** what happened to the rocks.

sandpaper

2 Put the rocks inside the jar of water. Close the lid tightly. Shake the jar for a few minutes.

plastic jar of water

3 Look at the rocks with a hand lens. **Communicate** what happened.

hand lens

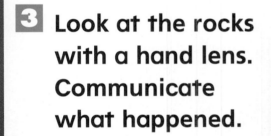

How can rocks change?

Water and wind can wear down rocks. **Erosion** happens when worn down rocks are carried away. It may happen so slowly that you can not see it.

When water or ice rubs against rock, it wears away at the rock. Water can move small rocks. These rocks bump into each other and break off into smaller pieces.

Grand Canyon,
Arizona

Wind can move sand. The sand rubs against rocks. The rubbing wears down the rocks bit by bit.

It has taken thousands of years for water and wind to wear down the rocks in these pictures.

▷ **Tell what happened to the rocks in these pictures.**

Monument Valley, Utah

Bryce Canyon, Utah

How can soil and sand change?

Bits of rock that wear away from bigger rocks become soil and sand. Bits of dead plants and animals also become part of soil.

Water can erode soil and sand. Heavy rain can wash soil away. Ocean waves can carry away sand.

Waves carry away sand.

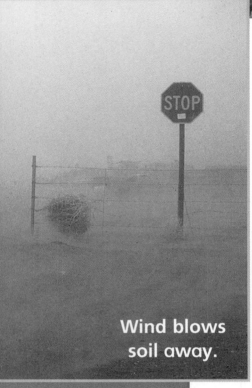

Wind blows soil away.

Wind can also erode soil and sand. Strong winds can blow soil and sand away. This may make a dust storm.

Plants help to keep soil and sand from eroding. Plant roots hold soil or sand in place. Then the weather cannot wash or blow soil or sand away easily.

How can plants help stop erosion?

Plants keep soil and sand in place.

Stop and Think

1. What is erosion?

2. Tell what soil is made of.

3. How can plants keep soil and sand from eroding?

HOME ACTIVITY Collect some rocks. Rub them together. Can any rocks be changed or scratched?

Earth Can Change Quickly

Get Ready

What happened to this road? What do you think might have caused this destruction?

Science Skill

You **observe** when you use your senses to learn about something.

Explore Activity

How can Earth's surface change?

What to do

1 Put the two halves of the pan together. Line it with foil. **BE CAREFUL!**

2 Make mud out of soil and water. Spread it in the pan. Wash your hands.

3 Let the mud dry in a warm place until it is hard.

4 Move the two sides of the pan quickly against each other.

5 **Observe** what happens. How did the surface change?

What you need

foil

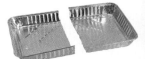
foil pan cut in half

bowl

water

soil

spoon

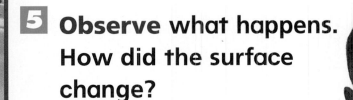

What is an earthquake?

An **earthquake** is a shaking of the ground. It is caused by a shift of Earth's surface, or crust. Earth's crust is made up of pieces called plates. These plates fit together like a puzzle. Sometimes the edges of two plates move or rub against each other. This can cause an earthquake.

▷ **How do earthquakes change Earth?**

An earthquake made this crack in the ground.

What is a landslide?

A **landslide** is a sudden movement of soil down a hill. Earthquakes sometimes cause landslides. Landslides may also happen when a lot of rainwater makes the soil heavy and slippery. The ground becomes weak and slides downhill.

▶ **How do landslides change Earth?**

What is a volcano?

A **volcano** is a mountain. It forms when hot, melted rock erupts through a hole in Earth's surface and builds up. The melted rock that flows out of the volcano is called lava. Lava becomes hard rock when it cools.

Volcanoes often form in places where Earth's plates rub against each other.

▷ **How can a volcano change Earth?**

The volcano erupts. Hot gases, lava, and ashes erupt from a hole in Earth's crust.

Hot rock builds up.

Mount St. Helens
April 1980

Mount St. Helens
May 18, 1980

After the volcano erupts, the lava cools into hard rock.

Mount St. Helens
June 1980

Years later, the volcano is no longer active. Plants begin to grow back and wildlife returns.

Mount St. Helens
1990

Stop and Think

1. What happens to Earth's crust in an earthquake?

2. What is a volcano?

3. What happens when lava cools?

MORE TO READ

Read **Shake Rattle and Roll: The World's Most Amazing Earthquakes, Volcanoes, and Other Forces,** by Spencer Christian.

Make a Weather Center

Have you ever imagined what it's like to be a weather person? Find out!

Try This!

Make a weather calendar for the week. Each day measure the temperature outside. Also measure the amount of rainfall, and whether it is windy or not windy. Record what you observe on the calendar.

Make Your Own Rocks

The Southwestern United States is filled with beautiful rock formations. Read *Standing Up Country: A Land of Surprises* by Linnea Gentry to find out about some of them.

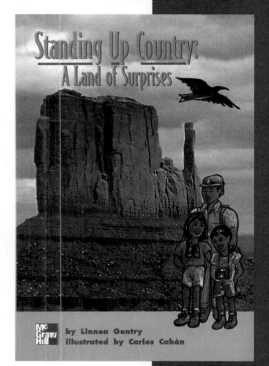

Standing Up Country: A Land of Surprises

by Linnea Gentry
illustrated by Carlos Cabán

Try This!

Use clay to make interesting rock shapes. They can look like the rocks in *Standing Up Country*. Or make shapes of your own.

Science Newsroom CD-ROM
Choose **The Water Cycle** to learn more about weather.

Vocabulary

condense

earthquake

erosion

evaporate

landslide

precipitation

volcano

water cycle

water vapor

Use each word once for items 1–9.

1 Water that goes into the air is called ____ .

2 Heat causes liquid water to ____ , or change into gas.

3 Rain, snow, and hail are kinds of ____ .

4 Cool air makes water vapor ____ , or turn into liquid water.

5 Water moving between the ground, sky, and back again is called the ____ .

6 When water or wind slowly wear something down, it is called ____ .

7 A shaking of the ground caused by the shifting of Earth's crust is an ____ .

8 A mountain made of cooled lava is a ____ .

9 A sudden movement of soil down a hill is a ____ .

Science Ideas

10 Which picture shows a drought?

A   **B**

11 What happens after precipitation falls from the sky?

Science Skill: Draw a Conclusion

12 Draw a conclusion about how these rocks got their shapes.

READ
California Fire! by Sneed B. Collard III

Earth
Yesterday and Today

Vocabulary

fossil
paleontologist
skeleton
extinct
endangered

Did You Ever Wonder?

How do we know what insects looked like in the time of dinosaurs? Whole insects have been found trapped in ancient tree sap. What kind of insect does this look like?

Clues in Rocks

Get Ready

Do you like to find clues? Look at these animal tracks. What kind of animal do you think made them? How do you know?

Science Skill

You **infer** when you use what you know to figure something out.

Explore Activity

How can we get clues from prints?

What to do

1 Flatten a piece of clay. Press a secret object into it. Gently take the object away.

2 Make prints with two more objects.

3 Trade clay prints with a partner. **Infer** what objects made the shapes. What clues did you use to figure them out?

What you need

clay

small objects

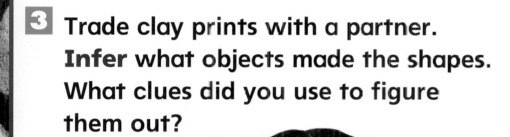

What are fossils?

Fossils are what is left of living things from the past. Some fossils are prints of plants or animals. Other fossils are parts of things that were once living. These parts can be bones or teeth. Fossils can also be footprints, tracks, or nests that animals left behind.

dinosaur footprint in rock

plant fossil in rock

dinosaur tooth fossil

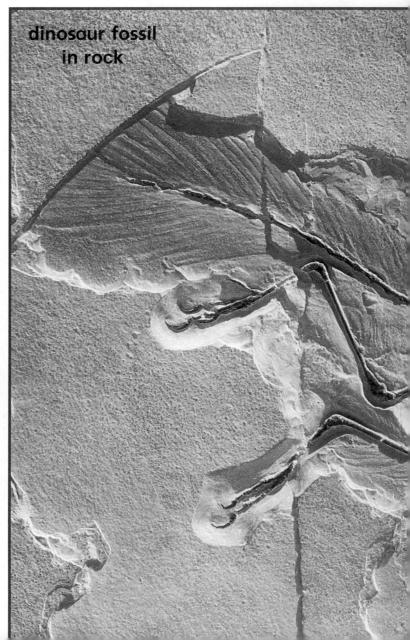

dinosaur fossil in rock

Scientists find fossils in many places. Many fossils are found in rock. A fossil may even be a whole animal or plant trapped and saved in ice, tar, or amber. Amber is hardened tree sap.

▷ **What are some different kinds of fossils?**

insect fossil in amber

saber-toothed cat fossil covered in tar

How are fossils formed?

Many fossils form when living things are buried. Most fossils are found in rocks that form very slowly in layers. Scientists can tell how old a fossil is when they know the age of the rock layer it is in.

 Where are most fossils found?

How a Fossil Forms

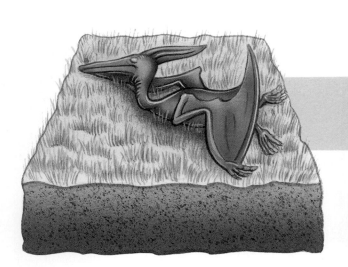

1 An animal dies. Layers of mud, soil, or clay bury the remains of the animal.

2 More mud layers build up. The soft parts of the animal rot away. The hard bones and teeth are left.

Stop and Think

1. What are fossils?

2. Tell how some fossils form.

3. Do you think fossils are still being formed today? Tell why or why not.

HOME ACTIVITY Press your hand into clay. Let the clay dry. What does the hand print tell about you?

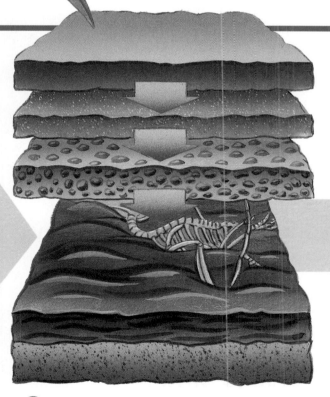

3 The mud, bones, and teeth slowly change to rock. The hard parts of the animal are saved.

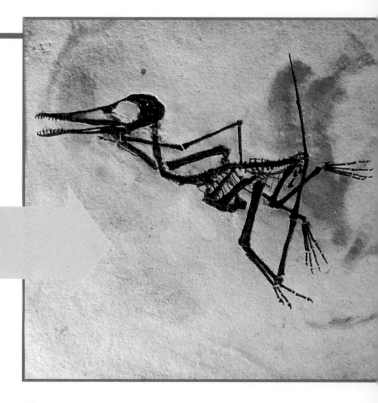

4 Millions of years later, the fossil is found.

Putting the Clues Together

Get Ready

Have you ever worked on a puzzle? Scientists work on puzzles, too. They put together fossil bones to show what an animal looked like.

Science Skill

You **make a model** when you build something that shows what the real thing is like.

Explore Activity

Which bones fit together?

scissors

What to do

1 Cut out the bones.

BE CAREFUL! Scissors are sharp.

tape

2 Make a **model** of a dinosaur. Fit the bones together.

3 Tape the bones together. Then tape them to a sheet of paper.

large sheet of paper

4 Tell how you put the pieces together.

dinosaur bone cutouts

How do scientists work with fossils?

Paleontologists are scientists who study things that lived long ago. They find and study fossils.

1 Scientists uncover fossils from rock.

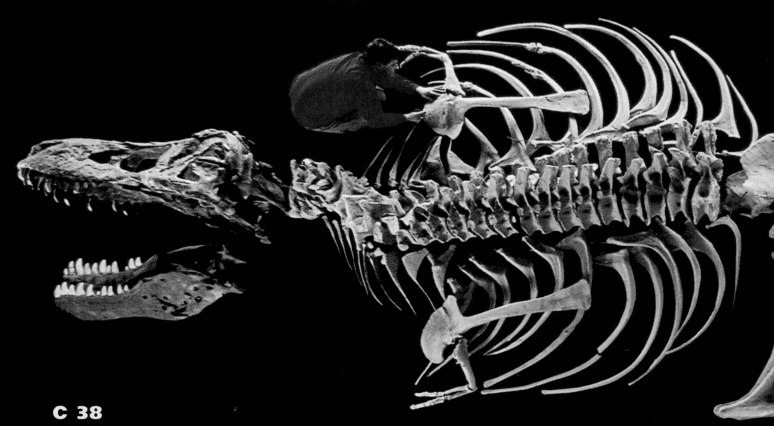

C 38

Scientists put together a dinosaur **skeleton**, or a full set of bones. Skeletons help scientists learn about animals. They can tell how big the animal was and how the animal may have moved.

▷ **What can this fossil skeleton tell us about the dinosaur?**

② They clean the fossil pieces. They rebuild some fossil bones from broken pieces.

③ Scientists put the fossil skeleton together.

Skeleton of Tyrannosaurus Rex

What clues do scientists get from animals today?

No one knows for sure what dinosaurs were like. So scientists use what they know about animals today. They compare fossil bones to the bones of living animals. This helps them put fossil bones together. It also helps them figure out how the animals may have lived and found food.

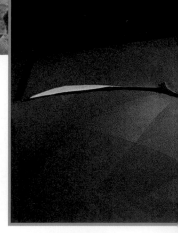

pterodactyl

stegosaurus

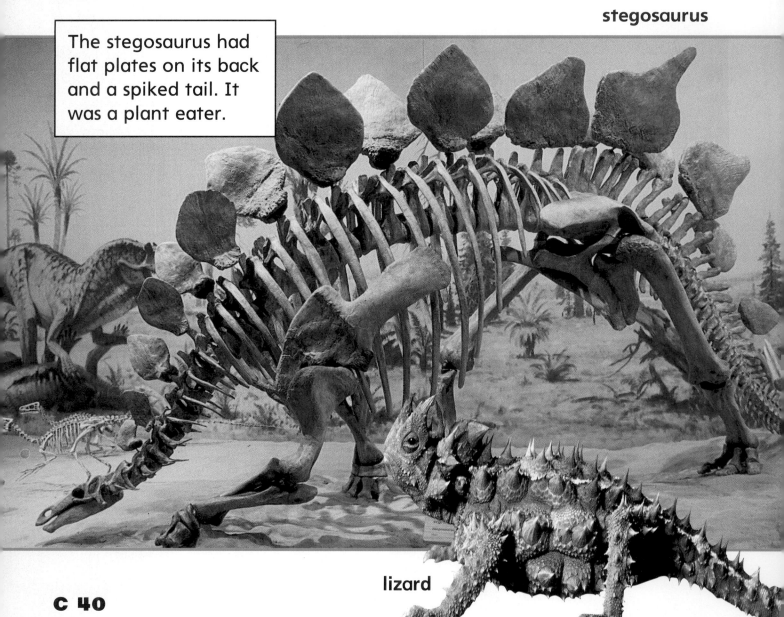

The stegosaurus had flat plates on its back and a spiked tail. It was a plant eater.

lizard

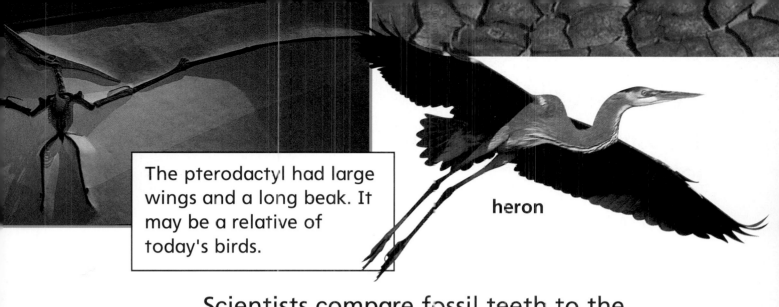

The pterodactyl had large wings and a long beak. It may be a relative of today's birds.

heron

Scientists compare fossil teeth to the teeth of animals today. They know that today's meat eaters have sharp teeth. They also know that today's plant eaters have flat teeth. This helps scientists figure out what dinosaurs ate.

allosaurus

The allosaurus was a predator. It had sharp claws, a large jaw, and long, sharp teeth.

?▶ Tell how these dinosaurs are like some animals of today.

alligator

How did dinosaurs live?

Dinosaurs lived on Earth millions of years ago. Some lived on land. Some dinosaurs flew.

Earth was very different then. The air and oceans were warm. The land had many swamps and giant forests.

pterodactyl

apatosaurus

allosaurus

Fossil footprints show that some dinosaurs lived in groups. This helped them to stay safe or hunt other animals. Tracks can show the kinds of prey meat-eating dinosaurs chased.

Some dinosaurs laid eggs. Scientists have found fossil nests. The nests had fossil eggs and young dinosaurs in them.

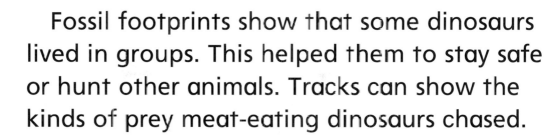

> **How do we know that dinosaurs laid eggs?**

stegosaurus

Stop and Think

1. Why are dinosaur bones like pieces of a puzzle?

2. What can fossil teeth tell us about an animal?

3. Why did some dinosaurs travel in groups?

MORE TO READ

Read **A Dinosaur Named Sue: The Find of a Century** by Fay Robinson.

6 Life on Earth Changes

Get Ready

A giant panda needs to eat up to 20 pounds of bamboo a day. That's as much as 60 heads of lettuce! What do you think would happen if a panda could not find any bamboo?

Science Skill

You **infer** when you use what you know to figure something out.

Explore Activity

What you need

index cards labeled Food, Water, or Shelter

What happens when animals can not meet their needs?

What to do

1 Line up with the class. Take three cards from the top of the pile.

2 If the three cards say Food, Water, and Shelter, go to the back of the line. If you are missing one of these cards, sit down.

3 Play for four more rounds.

4 What happens to the number of players each round? **Infer** what happens to animals when they can not meet their needs.

Why do living things become extinct?

When something is **extinct**, it has died out. That means none of its kind is living anywhere on Earth. Animals become extinct if they can not get the food, water, or shelter they need.

Long ago, many living things died out. They may have become extinct because of disease or big changes on Earth.

This is a drawing of a saber-toothed cat. It became extinct eleven thousand years ago.

This is a model of a triceratops. This dinosaur lived on Earth millions of years ago.

Today living things still become extinct. Many times people are the cause. People destroy habitats by cutting down forests and building on land where animals make their homes. People also hunt animals.

The dodo, shown in this drawing, became extinct in 1681.

? **Why are these animals extinct?**

This is a model of a woolly mammoth. The mammoth lived 20 thousand years ago.

The golden toad, last seen in 1989, is thought to be extinct.

pitcher plant

white rhinoceros

aye aye

What living things are endangered?

When living things are **endangered**, they are in danger of becoming extinct. They need to be kept safe in order to live. Today it is against the law to harm an endangered animal or plant.

We can help these animals and plants. We can keep the places where they live safe and clean.

manatee

lowland gorilla

▶ **Why are these living things endangered?**

Why is there hope for endangered life?

Some plants and animals have come back from near extinction. Some animals, such as the American bison, the bald eagle, and the humpback whale, are growing in numbers. This is because people have tried to keep the habitats of these animals safe. People have also stopped hunting them.

American bison

bald eagle

▶ **Why is it important to protect all habitats?**

humpback whale

Stop and Think

1. What may have caused dinosaurs to become extinct?

2. How do animals become endangered?

3. What can we do today to save endangered animals?

AT THE COMPUTER

Visit **www.mhscience02.com** to find out more about extinct and endangered animals.

Make a Dinosaur Big Book

Do you have a favorite dinosaur? Find a book about dinosaurs. Pick one you would like to learn about.

Try This!

Draw a picture of a dinosaur on a big piece of paper. Write facts about it. Then join with others to make a big book.

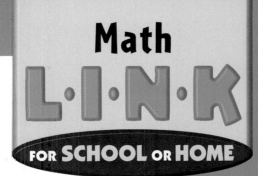

Collect and Sort Rocks

Rocks come in all shapes and sizes. Collect rocks and find out how many ways you can sort them.

small

medium

large

Try This!

Spread the rocks out on a table. Find three ways to describe your rocks. Then sort them. Record how many rocks are in each group.

Science Newsroom CD-ROM
Choose **Dino Match** to learn more about dinosaurs.

Chapter 6 Review

Vocabulary

| |
| endangered |
| extinct |
| fossils |
| paleontologist |
| skeleton |

Use each word once for items 1–5.

1 A scientist who studies living things from the past is a _____ .

2 Living things that have died out and no longer live on Earth are _____ .

3 Living things that are close to becoming extinct are _____ .

4 Remains of living things from the past are _____ .

5 A full set of bones is a _____ .

Science Ideas

6 How might this fossil have formed?

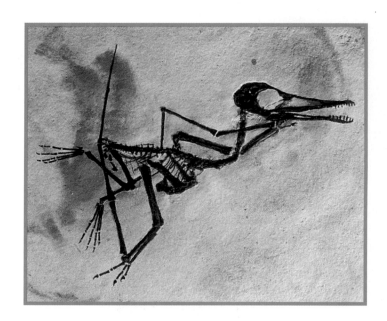

7 How are the animals in these pictures alike and different?

8 What can you infer from the shapes of this dinosaur's teeth?

READ
Saving Our Animals by Billy Goodman

Ji Qiang

Geologist

Ji Qiang (ZHEE CHAHNG) is a geologist. He studies rocks and the history of our Earth. He studied the fossils of a dinosaur that had feathers. This model (below) shows how the fossil might have looked as a living dinosaur.

Animals may change over time to survive changes on Earth. Some dinosaurs may have grown feathers to keep warm. Qiang and other scientists keep looking for clues that can teach us more about animals of the past and how they lived.

Dinosaur fossil

Qiang (center) studies a dinosaur fossil.

 Imagine you could talk to Qiang. What would you ask him about dinosaurs?

S C I E N C E
Workshop

1. **Write a story** about an Earth change that you learned about. Be sure to answer these questions:

- Is it a fast change or a slow change?

- How does the change happen?

Make a cover for your story. Give your story a title.

2. **Make a model** of a dinosaur and its habitat. Choose any dinosaur you want. Use a shoe box to make your model. Show what kind of teeth your animal has. Show the other animals and the plants that live near it.

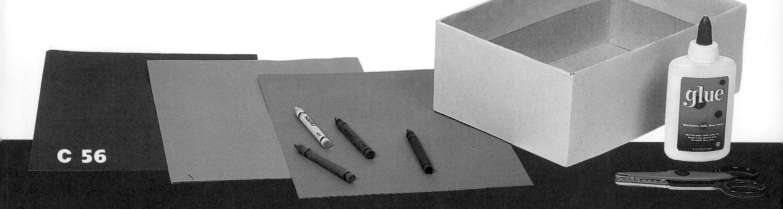

Earth Science

UNIT D
The Sun and Its Family

The Sun and Its Family

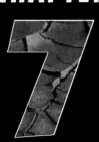

The Sun and Earth

Vocabulary

rotate

axis

Sun

orbit

equator

Did You Ever Wonder?

What would Earth be like without the Sun? It would be so dark and so cold that nothing would be able to live. How is the Sun a part of your life?

1 Day and Night

Atlanta at night

Get Ready

How are these two pictures different? How does day change to night? What kind of model could you make to show how this happens on Earth?

Science Skill

You make a model when you show how something happens.

Atlanta during the day

Explore Activity

How does day change to night?

What you need

foam ball

unsharpened pencil

paper clip

flashlight

What to do

1 Make a **model** of Earth. Push the pencil through the ball. **BE CAREFUL!**

2 Press the paper clip into one side of the ball.

3 Have a partner shine the flashlight at the paper clip. Where is it day on your model?

4 Slowly spin the ball with the pencil. What happens to the paper clip? Tell how this model shows how day changes to night.

How does Earth rotate?

Earth **rotates**, or spins, like a top. You can't feel it, but it is happening right now. Earth always spins in the same direction.

Earth rotates on a line through its center called an **axis**. Earth's axis is an imaginary line that goes from the North Pole to the South Pole.

axis

model of Earth

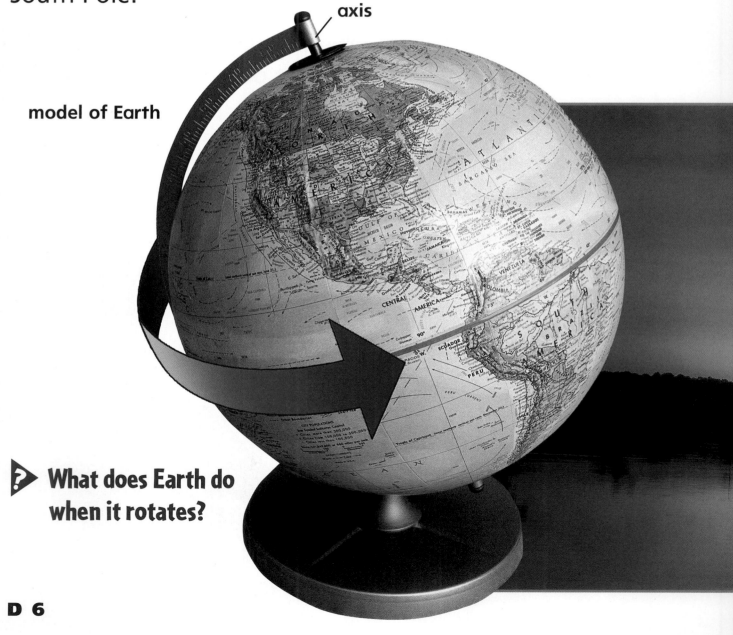

▶ **What does Earth do when it rotates?**

What is the Sun like?

As Earth rotates, the **Sun** shines on it. The Sun is a star. It is the closest star to Earth. The Sun gives Earth light and heat.

The Sun is huge. More than a million Earths could fit inside of it. The Sun looks small because it is 93 million miles away.

▷ **What does Earth get from the Sun?**

Sun

day in the United States

What causes day and night?

It seems as if the Sun is always moving across the sky. It looks as if the Sun rises in the east and sets in the west. But the Sun does not move. Earth's rotation causes day and night.

As Earth rotates, our part of Earth gets light, then dark. The Sun always shines, but it only lights half of Earth at a time. The half facing the Sun has light. The other half is dark. It takes 24 hours for Earth to rotate all the way around.

night in the United States

When it is daytime in the United States, what time of day is it on the other side of Earth?

Stop and Think

1. Why does the Sun look small?

2. What happens when Earth rotates?

3. How long does it take Earth to rotate one full time?

AT THE COMPUTER

Visit **www.mhscience02.com** to learn more about day and night.

Seasons

Get Ready

The same place can have different weather at different times of the year. Which picture shows Earth getting more light and heat from the Sun?

Science Skill

You **compare** when you observe how things are alike and different.

Explore Activity

How does Earth move through the year?

What you need

scissors

crayons

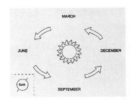

Sun worksheet

What to do

1 Color the Sun yellow on your worksheet. Color the Earth blue.

2 Cut out the picture of Earth along the dotted lines.

BE CAREFUL! Scissors are sharp.

3 Move Earth along the arrows on the page.

4 **Compare** where Earth is during different months of the year. How does Earth move during the year?

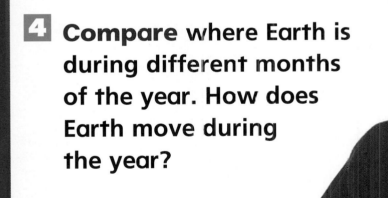

What causes the seasons?

As Earth rotates, it also moves in an **orbit** around the Sun. An orbit is the path an object takes as it moves around another object. Earth always moves in the same orbit. It takes Earth 365 days, or one year, to orbit the Sun.

fall

winter

summer

spring

Earth's axis leans a little to one side. Because of this, half of Earth is always tilted toward the Sun. As Earth orbits the Sun, different parts of Earth tilt toward the Sun. This causes the seasons to change.

▶ **Why do the four seasons come in the same order every year?**

fall

Why do seasons change?

When we have winter, our part of Earth tilts away from the Sun. Sunlight hits our part on a slant. So our part of Earth gets less light and heat.

winter

summer

When we have summer, our part of Earth tilts toward the Sun. The Sun is higher in the sky. So our part of Earth gets more light and heat.

▶ **Why does our part of Earth get less light and heat in winter?**

spring

What are seasons like in other places?

The **equator** is an imaginary line across the middle of Earth. It separates the northern part of Earth from the southern part. When it is summer in the northern part of Earth, it is winter in the southern part.

June 21st

United States, North America

June 21st

Argentina, South America

equator

Places near the equator do not have very different seasons. They have the same weather most of the year. This is because the Sun is high in the sky every day at the equator.

June 21st

Venezuelan rain forest near the equator

▷ **What will the seasons be like in each place in December?**

Stop and Think

1. What is an orbit?

2. Why does one part of Earth get more light and heat in the summer?

3. When it is winter in the northern part of Earth, what season is it in the southern part?

MORE TO READ

Read **Learn About the Changing Seasons** by Dr. Heidi Gold-Dworkin.

Go on a Sunset Walk

Sunsets can be beautiful! Read *Sunset Surprise* by Gail Tuchman.

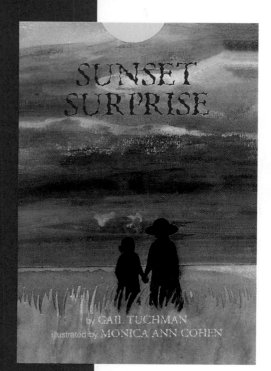

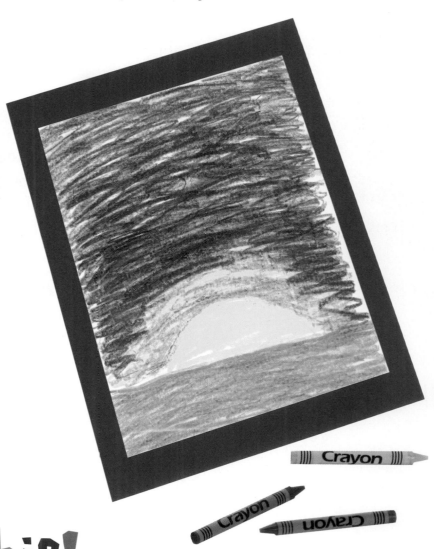

Try This!

With an adult, find a place where you can watch the sunset. Take a watch along. How long is it from the time the Sun begins to set until it is dark? Draw a picture of what you see.

Measuring Shadows

Did you know that shadows can tell you about the time of day? Shadows have different lengths depending on where the Sun is in the sky.

Try This!

Try measuring your shadow. Stand in exactly the same place at different times during the day. Have a friend or family member mark the top of your shadow with chalk. Measure how long it is each time. Record the numbers on a graph.

Chapter 7 Review

Vocabulary

axis
equator
orbit
rotates
Sun

Use each word once for items 1–5.

1 The closest star to Earth is the ____ .

2 Once every 24 hours, Earth spins around, or ____ .

3 A line through a spinning object is called an ____ .

4 The path an object takes as it moves around another object is an ____ .

5 The imaginary line that separates the northern part of Earth from the southern part is the ____ .

Science Ideas

6 What makes the Sun look as if it is rising and setting?

7 This place has the same weather most of the year. Where is it near?

Science Skill: Make a Model

8 This ball is a model of Earth. The paper clip shows where you live. What is the flashlight a model of?

Moon, Stars, and Planets

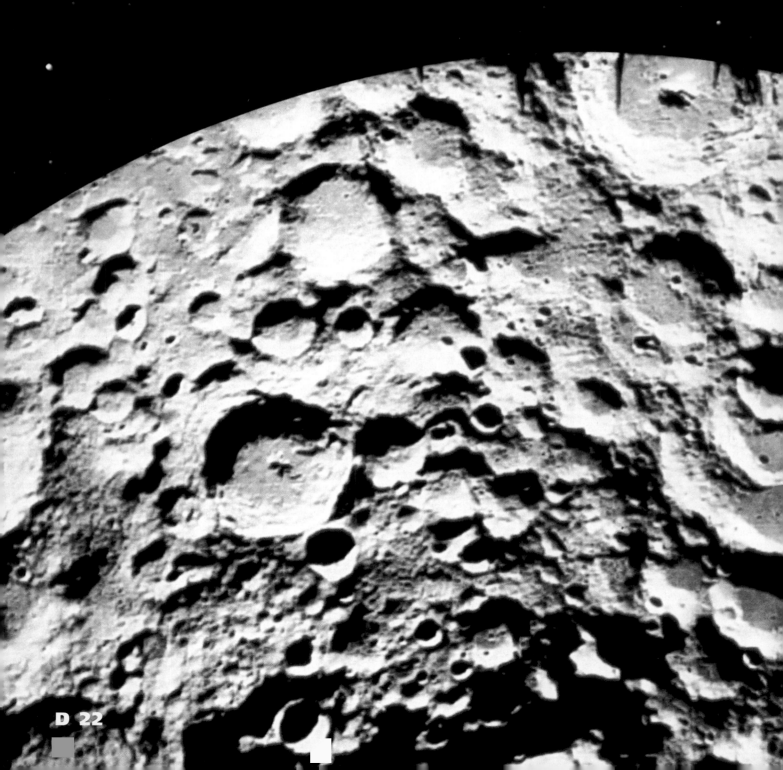

Did You Ever Wonder?

What does the surface of the Moon look like? It has big holes, mountains, and plains. The biggest hole is 183 miles wide. That would be about a three-hour car ride from end to end! What do you think caused these big holes?

The Moon

Get Ready

This picture was taken from space. It shows part of Earth and its nearest neighbor. What do you think that neighbor is? Why does it shine in the night sky?

Science Skill

You **infer** when you use what you know to figure something out.

Explore Activity

What makes moonlight?

What to do

1 Place a flashlight on a table. This is the Sun. Shine it at the large ball. This is Earth. Wrap the small ball in foil. This is the Moon.

2 Make the classroom dark except for the flashlight.

3 Move the Moon in a circle around Earth. Observe what makes the Moon shine. **Infer** what makes moonlight.

large foam ball

small foam ball

foil

flashlight

What is the Moon like?

The **Moon** is Earth's nearest neighbor. It is a ball of rock that orbits Earth. The Moon takes $29\frac{1}{2}$ days to make one full orbit.

The Moon is the brightest object in the night sky. But the Moon can not make its own light or heat. It looks like it shines because the Sun's light bounces off of it.

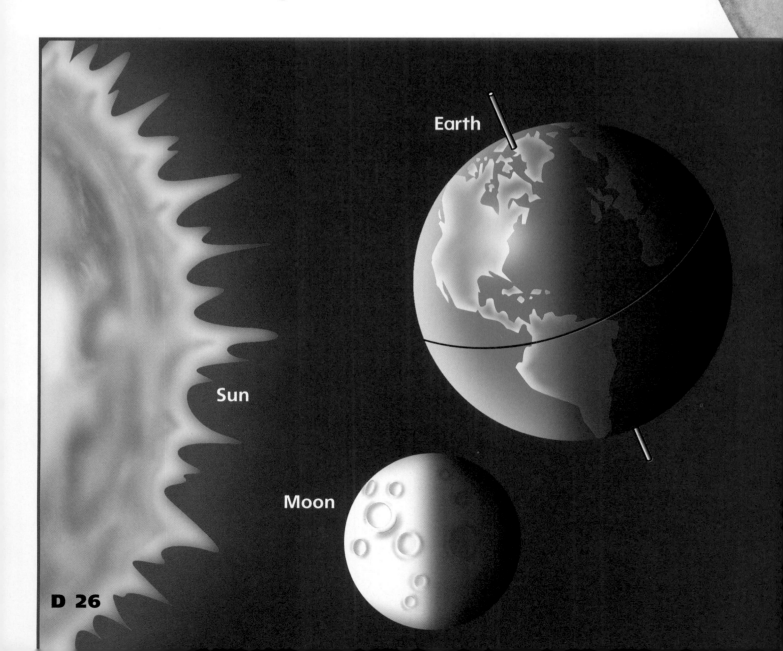

Earth

Sun

Moon

The Moon's surface is dry. It is covered with rocks and dust. The Moon has mountains and smooth areas. It also has many **craters**, or large holes. Most craters were made by rocks from space that crashed into the Moon.

 **Where does moonlight come from?**

What does the Moon look like during one night?

The Moon seems to move across the sky during the night. It rises in the east and sets in the west. Like the Sun, the Moon seems to move because Earth rotates. The Moon rises and sets as Earth turns.

7:30 P.M.

In early evening, the Moon is not very bright in the sky. Then the sky gets darker. The Moon seems to become brighter. The Moon looks brightest when the night sky is darkest.

11:00 P.M.

▶ **What makes the Moon look as if it is moving across the sky?**

Stop and Think

1. What is the Moon?

2. How does the Moon shine?

3. Why does the Moon seem to rise and set?

HOME ACTIVITY
Make Moon craters. Put flour on the bottom of a deep pan. Drop a few small rocks onto the pan.

The Moon Changes

Get Ready

Have you ever taken a good look at the night sky? Sometimes the Moon looks like a small sliver in the sky. Then, after a few days, it seems to look bigger. What do you think happens after that?

Science Skill

You put things **in order** when you tell what comes first, next, and last.

Explore Activity

How does the Moon change over time?

What to do

1 Look at the Picture Cards of the Moon.

2 Put the pictures in order. Start with the card that shows the least amount of the Moon.

3 Tell what the Moon looks like from the first card to the last.

4 What do the cards tell you about how the Moon changes over time?

What happens as the Moon seems to get bigger?

The Moon does not really get bigger and change shape. The part of the lit Moon that we can see changes. The different shapes of the Moon that we can see as it orbits Earth are called **phases**.

The first phase is the new Moon. We can not see the new Moon because its lit side is turned away from Earth.

April 30
new Moon

May 4
crescent Moon

Each night after the new Moon, we can see more of the Moon. After about 7 nights, the Moon is about one-fourth of the way through its orbit. We can see half of the Moon's lit side.

After about 14 nights, we can see a full Moon. When the Moon is full, Earth is between the Sun and the Moon. We can see all of the Moon's lit side.

▶ **Why can't we see the new Moon?**

May 7
first quarter

May 11

May 15
full Moon

What happens as the Moon seems to get smaller?

Each night after the full Moon, we see less of the Moon. After about 21 nights, the Moon is three-fourths through its orbit. We can see the other half of the Moon's lit side.

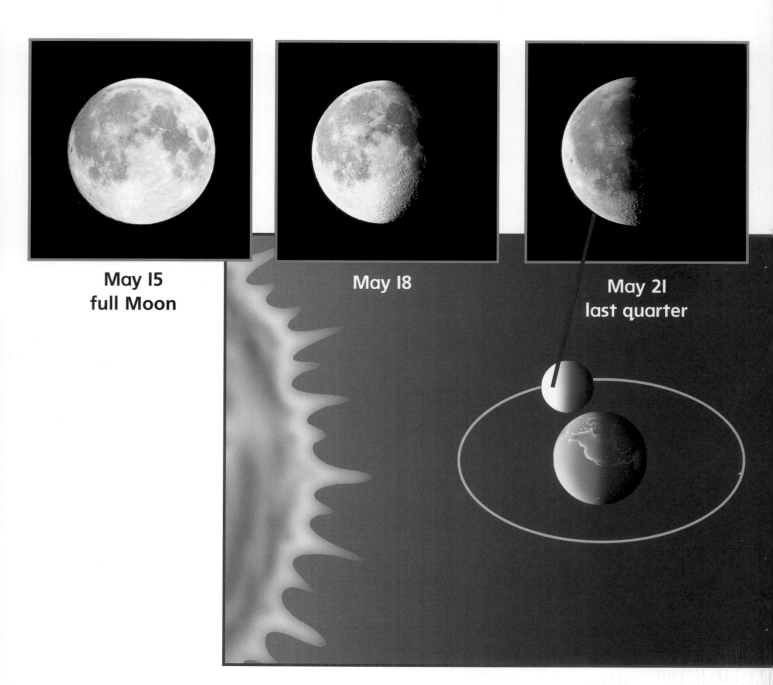

May 15
full Moon

May 18

May 21
last quarter

After about a month, the Moon seems to disappear again. It is the new Moon phase. It takes about a month for the Moon to change from a new Moon to full Moon and back again.

▶ **What happens after we see the next new Moon?**

May 25

**May 28
new Moon**

Stop and Think

1. Why do we see different shapes of the Moon?

2. What seems to happen to the Moon's shape right after the new Moon?

3. In which phase is the Moon closest to the Sun?

 **AT THE COMPUTER**   Visit **www.mhscience02.com** to learn more about the Moon.

5 Stars

Get Ready

The night sky is filled with stars. Look at the stars in this picture. Are some stars brighter than others? Are some stars bigger than others?

Science Skill

You **observe** when you use your senses to learn about something.

Explore Activity

What does the night sky look like?

cereal box

black paper

tape

flashlight

scissors

What to do

1 Wrap a box in black paper. Carefully poke holes on one side of the box to show part of the night sky.

BE CAREFUL! Handle scissors carefully.

2 Cut a hole in one end of the box. Shut off the lights. Shine a flashlight into the box.

3 Observe your box and share with others. How does the box look like the night sky?

What are stars?

A **star** is a hot ball of gases. Stars look tiny because they are so far away. The biggest stars are many times bigger than our closest star, the Sun.

When stars appear in the night sky, they seem to move from east to west as Earth rotates. There are too many stars to count! Scientists learn about stars by looking at them through tools called telescopes.

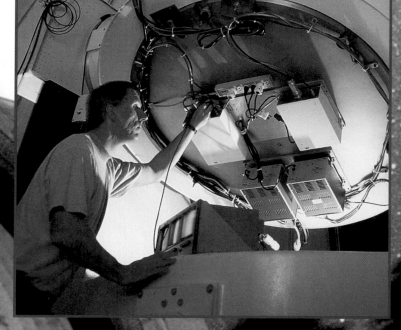

telescope

Stars may have different sizes and brightness. They may look bright because they are bigger or hotter than other stars near them. Stars also look bright when they are closer to Earth.

Stars have different colors. The hottest stars are blue. The coolest stars are red.

▷ **How many stars are there in the sky?**

blue star   red star

What are constellations?

People long ago saw that stars in the night sky formed pictures. They gave some of them names. A **constellation** is a star pattern that makes a picture.

Constellations are named after animals, objects, and people from old stories. There are 88 constellations in the sky.

Scorpius looks like a scorpion to some people.

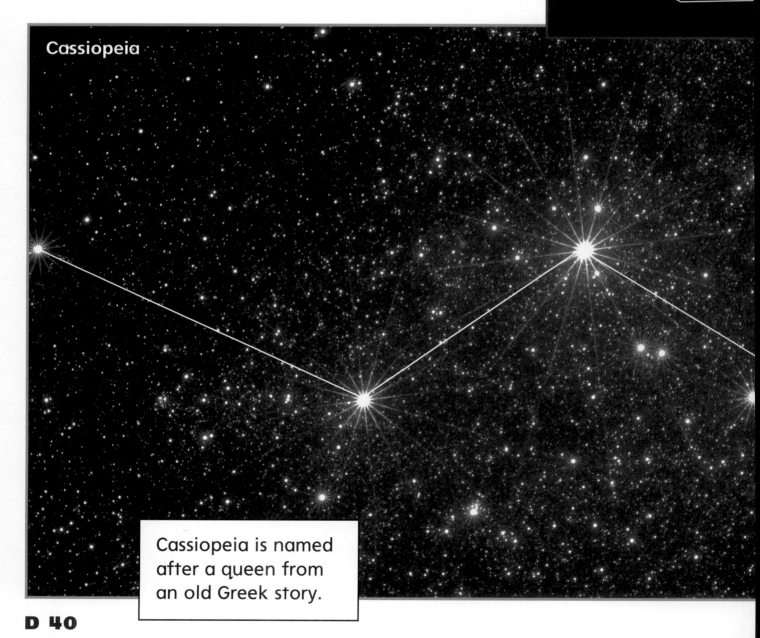

Cassiopeia

Cassiopeia is named after a queen from an old Greek story.

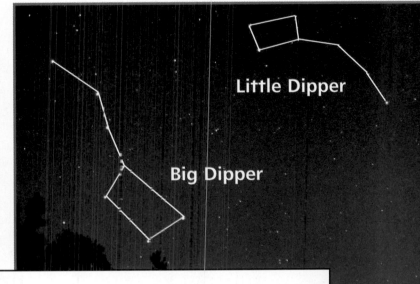

Scorpius

Little Dipper

Big Dipper

The Big Dipper and Little Dipper got their names because they are shaped like tools that hold water.

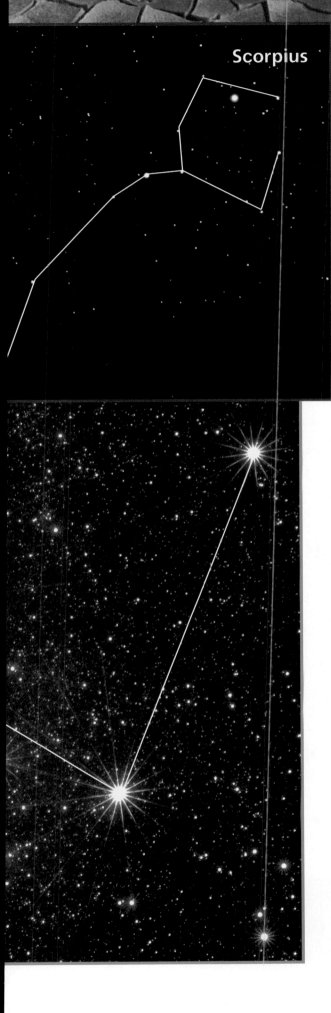

How did constellations get their names?

Stop and Think

1. Why do some stars look brighter than others?

2. What can you use to see objects in the night sky more clearly?

3. What is a constellation?

MORE TO READ

Read **The Night Sky (One Small Square)** by Donald M. Silver.

Planets

Get Ready

This is Jupiter. It takes about 12 Earth years for this planet to orbit the Sun! How could you show how Jupiter moves in space?

Science Skill

You make a model when you make something to show a place or thing.

Explore Activity

How are orbits alike and different?

chair

masking tape

string

What to do

1 Work in a group. Put a chair, labeled Sun, in the center of an empty room.

2 Tape a line from the chair to a wall. Place numbers I to 9 in order along the tape. Have each person line up on a number.

3 Make a **model** of an orbit. Each person walks in a circle around the chair. Take the same-size steps. Count your steps together.

4 Who gets back to the tape first? How were the orbits alike and different?

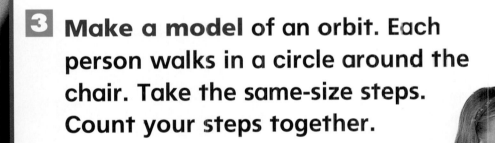

What is the solar system?

The **solar system** includes the Sun, nine **planets**, and their moons. A planet is a huge object that travels around the Sun. It does not make its own light or heat. Each planet has its own orbit, or path, around the Sun.

Venus

Sun

Mercury

Earth

Mars

Saturn

Some planets orbit close to the Sun. Others orbit far away. The planets closer to the Sun take less time to orbit. The planets farther from the Sun have longer to travel. They take more time to orbit the Sun.

▷ **Which planet takes the least amount of time to orbit the Sun?**

Jupiter

Neptune

Uranus

Pluto

What are the planets like?

Scientists have put the planets into two groups. The first four planets orbit closest to the Sun. These are called the inner planets. They are all solid balls of rock.

Mercury
Mercury is the closest planet to the Sun. It is rocky and has many craters like our Moon.

Venus
Venus is covered in thick yellow clouds. These clouds trap the Sun's heat. This makes Venus the hottest planet.

Earth
Earth is the planet on which we live. It has water and air. Earth is the only place we know that has life. It has one moon.

Mars
Mars is a dry planet. It has a red, rocky surface. Space missions have traveled to Mars to look for signs of life. It has two moons.

Jupiter

Jupiter is the largest planet. It has clouds and rings of dust. Jupiter has 28 moons that we know of.

The outer planets are farthest from the Sun. Scientists think that some outer planets do not have solid surfaces.

Saturn

Saturn is nearly as big as Jupiter. It has large rings made of ice. It may have over 20 moons.

▷ **How are the inner planets alike?**

Uranus

Uranus is a blue-green color. It is very cold. Uranus has thin rings made of ice and dust. It has about 20 moons.

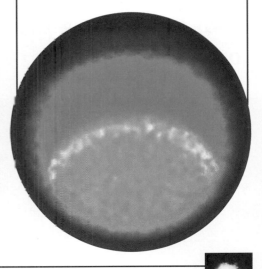

Neptune

Neptune is the blue planet. It has thin rings. Neptune has eight moons.

Pluto

Pluto is the smallest planet. It is the coldest. It has the longest orbit. Pluto is made of rock and ice. It has one moon.

How do we learn about the planets?

In 1957, *Sputnik*, the first spacecraft, was launched. Since then, thousands of spacecraft have traveled into space. Twelve people have also walked on the Moon. People who explore space are called astronauts.

Much of what we know about space comes from spacecraft called space probes. They carry tools that help us explore space and other planets.

These are pictures the Hubble Space Telescope has taken and sent back to us.

In 1997, the space probe *Mars Pathfinder* landed on Mars. It had a remote control robot that was controlled by someone on Earth. It took pictures and collected rocks.

The *Galileo* is a space probe that helps us learn about Venus and Jupiter.

▷ **What is a space probe?**

This astronaut is fixing the Hubble Space Telescope. This telescope takes pictures of things that are too far away for us to see from Earth.

Stop and Think

1. How many planets are in our solar system?

2. Which planet has the shortest orbit? the longest orbit?

3. What are some ways we learn about space?

MORE TO READ Read **Children of the Sun** by Arthur John L'Hommedieu.

Draw the Night Sky

Look at the night sky on a clear night. Do you see any constellations? Can you tell what phase the Moon is in?

Try This!

Draw what you see in the night sky. Use black paper and white chalk or crayons. You can draw pictures at different times of the month. Compare what you see.

Star Stories

There are many stories about how people long ago thought the night sky came to be. Some stories tell why the Moon changes shape. Others tell why some stars shine brighter than others.

Why the North Star is so Bright

Try This!

Write a story about the night sky. Use your imagination to tell why the stars and planets are in the sky. Then draw pictures for your story.

 Science Newsroom CD-ROM Choose **Constellations** to learn more about the night sky.

Chapter 8 Review

Vocabulary

constellation
craters
Moon
phases
planet
solar system
star

Use each word once for items 1–7.

1 A large ball of rock that orbits Earth is the ____ .

2 Large holes in the Moon caused by space rocks are ____ .

3 The different shapes that the Moon seems to have as it orbits Earth are called ____ .

4 A hot ball of gases is a ____ .

5 A star pattern that makes a picture is a ____ .

6 A huge object that travels around the Sun is a ____ .

7 The Sun, nine planets, and their moons make up the ____ .

Science Ideas

8 Tell how we learn about the night sky.

9 As planets get farther from the Sun, what happens to their orbits?

10 Look at the pictures from left to right. Predict what will come next. Draw a picture.

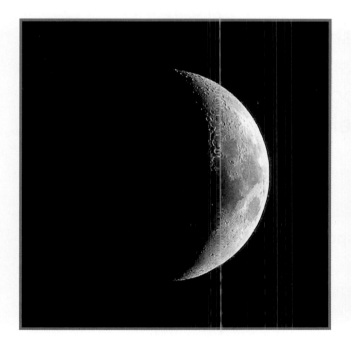

Mae Jemison
Astronaut

Did you ever dream of flying into space? Mae Jemison did. Her dream came true. She became an astronaut. Astronauts explore space. Mae was the first African-American woman in space.

Before Mae became an astronaut, she was a doctor. But more than anything, she wanted to be part of America's space team.

In 1992, Mae blasted off into space aboard a space shuttle. In space, she and the crew tested how flies, hornets, fish, frogs, and humans behave while weightless.

Astronauts fly into space in a space shuttle.

Mae Jemison inside the space shuttle *Endeavour*

Imagine you were in space with Mae. Write about what you did and how you felt.

SCIENCE
Workshop

1. **Draw a picture** of your favorite season. Show what you like to do outdoors. Be sure your picture shows:

   - what the weather is like
   - how you are dressed

   Write a sentence to tell why the weather is like it is.

2. **Imagine you are** a space explorer. If you could visit the Moon or any of the planets, where would you go? Why? Tell what you would do. Write a story about your trip. Draw pictures of what you would see.

Matter and Energy

Vocabulary

matter

mass

property

temperature

solid

liquid

volume

gas

physical change

chemical change

Did You Ever
Wonder?

How do these wind surfers use all three forms of matter? The surfboard is a solid. It floats on top of water. Air pushes the wind surfer forward. Have you ever used these three kinds of matter?

1 Matter All Around

Get Ready

Have you ever been to a party? Look at the party in this picture. What could you see, hear, smell, and touch? Tell about each one.

Science Skill

You **observe** when you use your senses to learn about something.

Explore Activity

How can you tell what is inside?

What to do

1 Observe each container without opening it.

2 Guess what is inside each one. Record your guess.

3 Open each container to see what is inside. What clues did you use to tell what was inside?

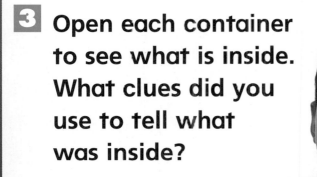

How are all things alike?

All things are made of **matter**. Matter is anything that takes up space. Observe the objects in this room. They are all made of matter. You are made of matter, too.

The air in these balloons is matter.

These stuffed animals are matter.

All matter also has **mass**. Mass is how much matter is in an object. A bed has a lot of mass. A goldfish has only a little mass.

? **How is everything in this room alike?**

This boy is matter.

This metal can is matter.

The water in this tank is matter.

How can you describe matter?

You can describe matter by its properties. A **property** tells you something about an object. Some properties of matter are shape, size, and color. Matter can sink or float. This is also a property.

big, soft

red, shiny

floats

sinks

hot

Temperature measures how warm something is. Temperature is a property of matter.

Texture tells the way something feels. Texture is another property of matter.

fuzzy   smooth

What are some other properties of this stuffed frog?

Stop and Think

1. What is matter?

2. Name something that has a lot of mass. Name something that has a little mass.

3. Name three properties of matter.

AT THE COMPUTER Visit **www.mhscience02.com** to learn more about matter.

Three States of Matter

Get Ready

Matter is everywhere! What kinds of matter do you see in this picture? Which things have the most mass? Which things have the least mass?

Science Skill

You put things **in order** when you tell what is first, next, and last.

Explore Activity

How can you put matter in order?

What you need

classroom objects

balance

What to do

1 Look at each object. Which has the most mass? Which has the least mass? Predict.

2 Compare two objects on the balance. The one that makes the pan go lower has more mass.

3 Put the objects in order from least mass to most mass.

What is a solid?

There are three different states of matter. **Solid** is one state of matter. Like all matter, a solid takes up space and has mass. But only a solid has a shape of its own. A crayon and a yo-yo are both solids.

yo-yo

in-line skate

Crayon

pocket game

feather

E 12

You can measure the shape of a solid. A ruler is a tool that measures how long, wide, or high things are. This ruler measures centimeters. Some rulers measure inches.

ruler

You can measure the mass of a solid. A balance is a tool that measures mass. The side of the balance that is lower holds the thing that has more mass.

balance

▶ **How are all of these objects alike?**

What is a liquid?

Liquid is another state of matter. A liquid takes up space and has mass. A liquid does not have a shape of its own. It takes the shape of its container. Milk, juice, and water are all liquids.

oil

liquid soap

milk

juice

Volume is the amount of space that something takes up. You can measure the volume of a liquid. A measuring cup is one way to measure volume. A measuring cup can hold the same amount of liquid every time.

▶ **How can you measure the volume of this punch?**

E 15

What is a gas?

The third state of matter is **gas**. It takes up space and has mass. Gas spreads out to fill its container. It does not have a shape of its own.

Air is made up of gases. You can not see it, but air is everywhere. It can fill up a tire or a ball.

kite

air pump
and tire

balloons

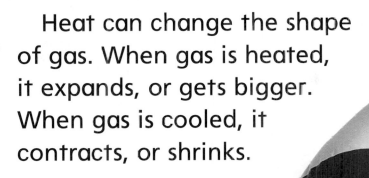
blimp

Heat can change the shape of gas. When gas is heated, it expands, or gets bigger. When gas is cooled, it contracts, or shrinks.

▶ **Where is gas in each of these pictures?**

Stop and Think

1. What are three states of matter?

2. What kind of matter is an ice cube?

3. What kind of matter is air?

MORE TO READ

Read **Solids, Liquids, and Gases** by Louise Osborne, Deborah Hodge, and Ray Boudreau.

Changing Matter

Get Ready

Have you ever put two or more things together to make something new? Look at this work of art. How would you make something like this?

Science Skill

You **investigate** when you make a plan and try it out.

Explore Activity

How can you change matter?

glue

paper

scissors

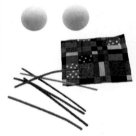

craft materials

What to do

1. Observe your objects. Think of ways to change them and put them together.

2. **Investigate** how to change and put together the objects. Make a plan and try it out.

   BE CAREFUL! Scissors are sharp.

3. What did you make? What did you do to make it? Tell about the different ways you changed matter.

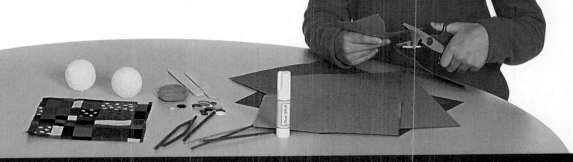

What is physical change?

Matter may change in different ways. You can change the size or shape of matter. This is called a **physical change**.

In a physical change, you can cut, fold, bend, or tear matter. When you only change the shape of matter, its mass stays the same.

You can also change matter by mixing it. A mixture is something made up of two or more different things.

Mixing is a physical change. When pieces of matter are mixed together, each piece is the same as it was before it was mixed.

The salad and salad dressing are both mixtures.

▷ **Which has more mass, a head of lettuce, or a head of lettuce torn into pieces?**

What is chemical change?

Sometimes matter can change into different matter. This is called a **chemical change**. Once matter goes through a chemical change, it is not the same as it was before. Burning matter is one way to make a chemical change.

Burning is a chemical change. It changes wood to ashes.

Rusting is a chemical change. Some metals can rust.

What happens after something goes through a chemical change?

All matter does not change in the same way. The air can change the color or shape of a fruit. An apple will turn brown. An orange will dry out.

Water and air can cause iron to rust, but the plastic will not change.

Before	After

Before	After

Stop and Think

1. Name a physical change.

2. What is a mixture?

3. Name a chemical change.

Visit **www.mhscience02.com** to learn more about how matter can change.

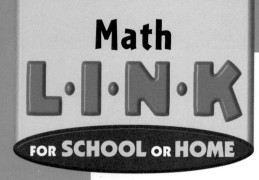

Math
L·I·N·K
FOR **SCHOOL** OR **HOME**

Measuring Mixtures

How do chefs know how much of each thing to use when they cook? They measure!

Try This!

Make a tasty trail mix. Use cereals and dried fruits to make a mixture. Use measuring cups to show how much of each thing you use. Then write a recipe card.

Use Chemical Changes to Write a Secret Note

Have you ever wanted to write a secret note? Now you can.

Try This!

Dip a cotton swab into a glass of milk or lemon juice. Write a message on white paper with the cotton swab. Let the note dry. Then hold the note up to a window on a sunny day. Watch to see what happens!

Chapter 9 Review

Vocabulary

chemical change

gas

liquid

mass

matter

physical change

property

solid

temperature

volume

Use each word once for items I–9.

1 Anything that takes up space and has mass is ____ .

2 The amount of matter in an object is called its ____ .

3 The size, shape, or color of an object is a ____ of the object.

4 Matter that has a shape of its own is called a ____ .

5 Matter, such as juice, that has no shape of its own is called a ____ .

6 The amount of space something takes up is called its ____ .

7 Matter, such as air, that spreads out to fill its container is called a ____ .

8 A measure of how warm something is shows ____ .

9 Write which type of change each picture shows.

A

B

Science Ideas

Tell what kind of matter each picture shows.

10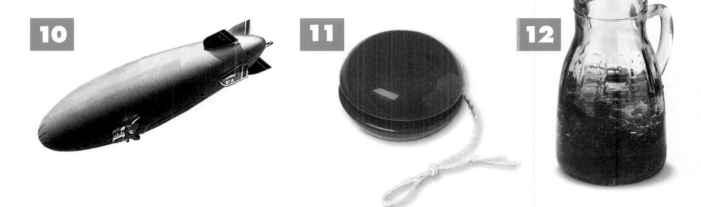

11

12

13 List the properties of the balloons.

Science Skill: Investigate

14 Write a plan for how you could change this clay by making only physical changes.

10 Energy

energy
heat
fuel
light
reflect
refraction
sound
vibrate
pitch

Did You Ever Wonder?

What happens when fireworks explode?
They make sound, light, and heat.
Sound, light, and heat are all forms of
energy. Can you name other things that
make sound, light, or heat?

Heat

Get Ready

A cold treat is great on a hot day. But the treat won't last long. Look at the picture. What do you think makes this ice cream lose its shape? Tell your ideas to a partner.

Science Skill

You **communicate** when you **share your ideas** with others.

Explore Activity

How can heat change matter?

What you need

paper plates

ice cube

butter

chocolate

What to do

1 Find a sunny spot outside on a warm day. Place the ice cube, the butter, and the chocolate on top of the paper plates. Draw how they look.

2 Do you think the Sun will change any of the items? Why or why not?

3 Leave the paper plates in the Sun for 20 minutes.

4 **Communicate** what happens to each item. Draw how they look. How did heat change matter?

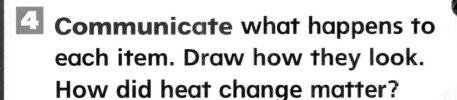

How can heat change matter?

Energy is the power to make matter move or change. One kind of energy is **heat**. Heat can change the state of matter. Taking away heat can make something freeze. Adding heat can make something melt or boil.

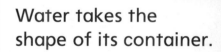

Water takes the shape of its container.

The tray is put in the freezer. The liquid will change to a solid state.

The solid ice cubes are placed in a pot and left at room temperature.

4 Heat causes the solid ice to melt, or become liquid.

5 The water returns to a liquid state.

6 When the water gets very hot, it boils. Then the liquid becomes a gas.

▶ **How can you change the state of water?**

How can we use heat?

We use heat every day. Much of our heat is from the Sun. The Sun warms Earth's land, air, and water. Without the Sun, Earth would become too cold for things to live.

Fire is one kind of heat. We can use fire to keep warm and to cook our food. To make heat, a fire needs to burn **fuel**. A fuel gives off heat when it burns. Wood, natural gas, and oil are fuels.

Heat can change some kinds of clay. When a potter puts a clay pot in a special oven, the clay changes. It becomes a different kind of matter that is very hard.

▶ How is heat used in these pictures?

Stop and Think

1. Name two ways heat can change matter.

2. Where does much of our heat come from?

3. What is fuel?

HOME ACTIVITY Put a tray of water and a wooden block in the freezer for two hours. What happens to each one?

Light

Get Ready

Look at the buildings in this picture. What do you see? What direction is the light coming from?

Science Skill

You **observe** when you use your senses to find out about something.

Explore Activity

How does light move?

flashlight

mirror

What to do

1 Work with a partner. Stand near a wall with the flashlight.

2 Your partner will stand a few feet away from you and hold the mirror.

3 Turn on the flashlight and shine it at the mirror. Your partner will try to make the light shine from the mirror onto the wall.

4 **Observe** what happens to the light. What did you find out about how light moves?

What is light?

Light is a kind of energy that lets us see. Light travels in straight lines.

When light hits an object, some of it **reflects,** or bounces off, the object. When light reflects off smooth, flat objects like mirrors, it bounces in one direction.

This mirror is not flat. When light hits the surface, it bounces off in many directions. This makes your reflection look funny.

How can you make a shadow? You can block light with an object. A shadow is the dark area that light does not reach.

Glass or water can bend light. This is called **refraction**. A hand lens bends light. Bending light can make something look bigger.

▷ **How does light travel?**

Light bends when it travels through this hand lens. Bent light makes the butterfly look bigger.

How do we use light?

Much of Earth's light is from the Sun. Living things need the energy from sunlight. Without the Sun, Earth would be in darkness. Nothing would be able to live or grow here.

People once used fire for light at night and indoors. Now we use electric lights to help us see.

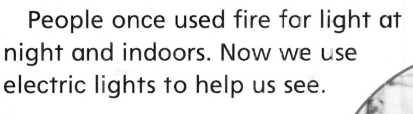

▶ **How is light energy being used in these pictures?**

Stop and Think

1. What is light?

2. How is a shadow made?

3. What gives us light energy after dark?

AT THE COMPUTER

Visit **www.mhscience02.com** to learn more about light.

Sound

Get Ready

Sounds are all around us. Look closely at this picture. How are these people making sound? What do you think it sounds like?

Science Skill

You **observe** when you use your senses to find out about something.

Explore Activity

paper cup

string

goggles

paper clip

How is sound made?

What to do

1 Work with two partners. Make a tiny hole in the bottom of the cup.

2 Tie the string to the paper clip. Pull the string through the hole until the clip is tight inside the bottom of the cup.

3 You and a partner hold the cup and string. A third partner snaps the string. **BE CAREFUL!** Wear goggles.

4 **Observe** what happens. How did you make sound?

What is sound?

Sound is a kind of energy that you hear. Sound is made when something **vibrates**, or moves back and forth. When something vibrates it makes the air vibrate, too. Vibrating air carries the sound you hear.

When you speak, air from your lungs makes your vocal chords vibrate. Touch your throat as you speak. Feel the vibration.

Sound travels in waves. Sound waves move through the air like ripples in a pond.

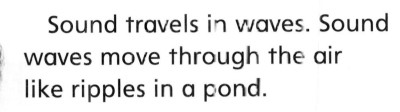

▷ **What carries most of the sound you hear?**

E 45

What is loudness?

Not all sounds are the same. Some sounds are loud. Big vibrations make loud sounds. Some sounds are soft. Small vibrations make soft sounds. The farther away you are from a sound, the softer it sounds to you.

▶ **How would you compare the sound of a motorcycle to the sound of a bicycle?**

What is pitch?

Sounds can also be high, low, or somewhere in between. **Pitch** is how high or how low a sound is.

Musical instruments work by vibrating. Look at this instrument. When you hit a small bar, the vibrations are fast. The pitch is high. When you hit a big bar, the vibrations are slow. The pitch is low.

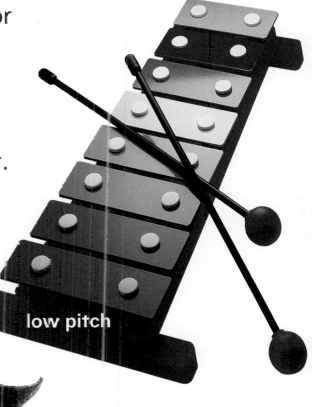

high pitch

low pitch

> **How would you describe the pitch of each dog's bark?**

What can sound move through?

Sound can move through gases, liquids, and solids. Most sound you hear is moving through air. Air is made of gases.

You can hear sounds underwater. The sounds make the water vibrate.

Have you put your ear to a desk or a door and heard a sound from the other side? The sound makes the wood vibrate. The wood is a solid.

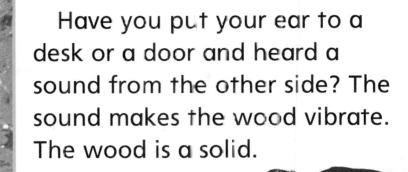

? **What happens when sound travels through a solid?**

Stop and Think

1. How is sound made?

2. What is pitch?

3. Tell what sound can move through.

MORE TO READ

Read **Energy** by Alvin Silverstein, Virginia Silverstein, and Laura Silverstein Nunn.

Thomas Alva Edison

by Tamera Bryant
illustrated by Laurie Jordan

McGraw Hill

Write About the Past

Think about what life was like before electric light bulbs. Read *Thomas Alva Edison* by Tamera Bryant. Think about all the things that Edison invented. How did they change people's lives?

Try This!

How would your life be different without Thomas Edison's inventions? Write a story about what your life might have been like.

Make Your Own Music

People have been making music for a very long time. The first instruments invented were probably hollow logs used as drums. You can invent your own instrument, too.

Try This!

Think of ways to make a musical instrument. Find things that can make sounds. Try to make sounds with high pitch and low pitch. Can you play a tune?

 Science Newsroom CD-ROM Choose **Bouncing Sounds** to learn more about sound.

E 51

Chapter 10 Review

Vocabulary

energy

fuel

heat

light

pitch

reflects

refraction

sound

vibrates

Use each word once for items 1–9.

1 The power to make matter move or change is called ____ .

2 Energy that can change the state of matter is called ____ .

3 Something that gives off heat when it burns is ____ .

4 Energy that you hear is called ____ .

5 How high or low a sound is, is called its ____ .

6 When something moves back and forth quickly, it ____ .

7 Energy that allows you to see is called ____ .

8 When light bounces off a mirror, the mirror ____ the light.

9 When something bends light, it is called ____ .

Science Ideas

10 What can sound move through?

11 Which picture shows heat?

A

B

C

Science Skill: Investigate

Tell what each of these pictures shows.

12

13

READ
Fossil Fuels Keep Us Warm by Shirley Granahan
Sending a Message with Dots...and Dashes... by Emily North

E 53

A GLOW-ING IDEA!

When Becky Schroeder was ten years old, she had a really bright idea. One afternoon, she was doing homework while in the car with her mom. Soon it got dark. Becky wanted to see what she was writing without turning on a light. So she invented a way to do it.

Becky Schroder has dreamed up nine inventions.... This is one of Them.

Becky Schroeder's Glo-sheet

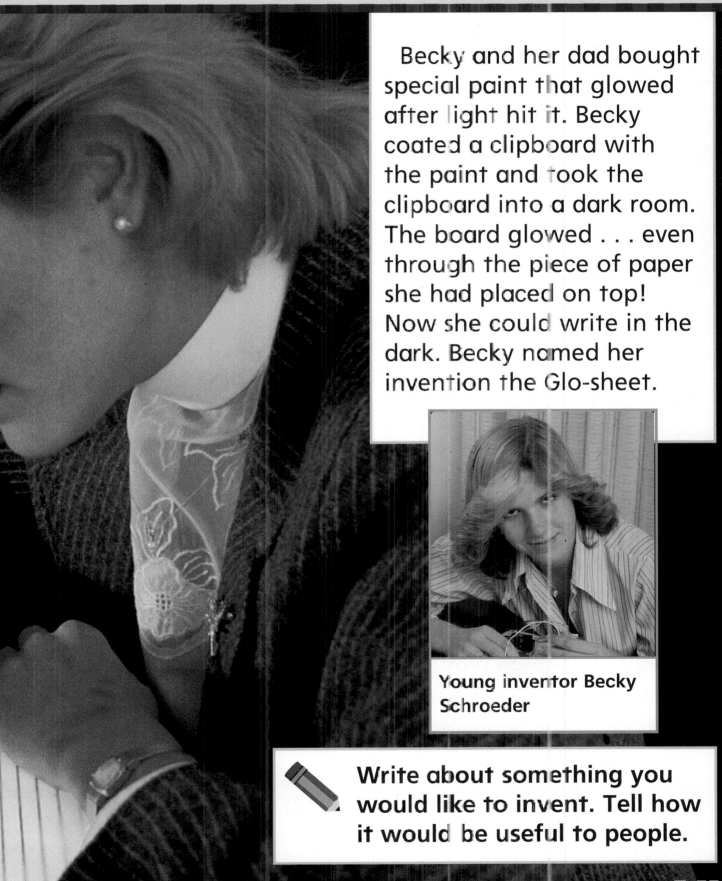

Becky and her dad bought special paint that glowed after light hit it. Becky coated a clipboard with the paint and took the clipboard into a dark room. The board glowed . . . even through the piece of paper she had placed on top! Now she could write in the dark. Becky named her invention the Glo-sheet.

Young inventor Becky Schroeder

Write about something you would like to invent. Tell how it would be useful to people.

SCIENCE
Workshop

1. **Matter, Matter Everywhere** Choose one of the objects shown. What state of matter is the object? What are its properties? How can you make a physical change to the object? How can you make a chemical change to the object? Make a booklet to show.

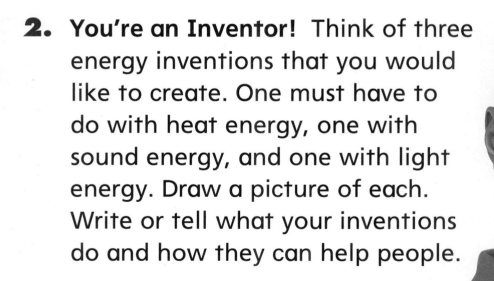

2. **You're an Inventor!** Think of three energy inventions that you would like to create. One must have to do with heat energy, one with sound energy, and one with light energy. Draw a picture of each. Write or tell what your inventions do and how they can help people.

Physical Science

UNIT

F Watch It Move

NATIONAL GEOGRAPHIC

Watch It Move

LOOK!

Snowboarding is like skateboarding without wheels! How does this snowboarder move forward? Take a good look.

11 Forces and Machines

Did You Ever Wonder?

What makes things move? Pushes and pulls make things move. Each part of this machine works together to do a job. Can you name any machines that use pushes and pulls?

Vocabulary

force

gravity

friction

simple machine

lever

fulcrum

ramp

Pushes and Pulls

Get Ready

Have you ever played with marbles?
They can move far if you give them
a push. How far can a marble move?

Science Skill

You **measure** when you find out
how far something moves.

Explore Activity

How far can different things move?

What to do

1 Mark a starting line with tape. Line up the objects.

2 Tap each object to make it move forward. Do not tap one thing harder than the others.

3 Measure how far each object moved. Use a ruler.

4 Record how far each object moved. Which object moved the farthest? Why do you think so?

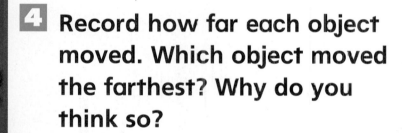

What makes things move?

Things can not move on their own. A push or a pull makes something move or change direction. A push or a pull is called a **force**.

When the man pulls the sled, he uses force to move it. When the adults push the girl, they use force to move her.

push

pull

Gravity is a force that pulls things toward Earth. When you go downhill, gravity makes you speed up. It also holds you back when you go uphill.

Gravity holds you on Earth. You can see the pull of gravity when you let go of an object. It falls toward Earth.

▷ **What kinds of movement do you see in these pictures?**

Gravity pulls things downhill.

How do objects move?

Objects can move in different ways. You can tell how objects move by the paths they make.

The roller coaster ride begins in a straight line. But soon it moves on a curved path. The swing ride moves in a circle.

circle

curved

back and forth

zigzag

This ride moves back and forth. Some things, like this ball, move in a zigzag. A zigzag is a path with short, sharp turns from one side to another.

▷ What makes these things move?

Stop and Think

1. How can you make something move?

2. What is gravity?

3. What are some ways objects can move?

HOME ACTIVITY Look around your home. Make a list of pushes and pulls that you see.

Forces and Change

Do you think this truck could go faster here or on a street? Why?

Science Skill

You **compare** when you tell how things are alike and different.

Explore Activity

How can you slow down a force?

What to do

1 Stack the books. Put the edge of the board on the books to make a hill.

2 Put the car at the top of the hill and let go. Do not push it. Place tape where the car stopped.

3 Cover the board with wax paper. Repeat step 2.

4 Try the activity again with sandpaper, then cloth.

5 Compare how far the car went each time. What slowed down the car most?

What you need

cardboard

3 books

toy bus

wax paper

sandpaper

cloth

tape

What slows things down?

Friction is a force that slows down moving things. It happens when two things rub together.

There is more friction on rough surfaces than on smooth ones. It is harder to push or pull something over a rough surface than over a smooth surface.

▶ **What force slows down the cart? The skater?**

When you skate, your wheels move along a surface. To stop, you drag a rubber stopper on the ground. You will slow down until you stop. This happens because dragging causes friction.

What happens when you change a force?

When a force changes, the way a thing moves changes, too. A little force can make a golf ball move slowly. More force can make the golf ball move faster and farther.

It takes more force to move some things than it does to move others. The heavier something is, the more force you need to move it.

▶ **Who is using more force to pull the luggage?**

How can force change motion?

When something moves, it is in motion. Forces can change the motion of things. When something standing still starts to move, its motion changes.

Speeding up, slowing down, and stopping are changes in motion, too. Pushing or pulling forces make these changes in motion.

The pushing force of the bowling ball changes the motion of the pins.

In a game of table tennis, you use a paddle to hit the ball across the net. Each hit is a push. The push changes the motion of the ball. The ball goes back and forth in different directions.

▶ **How does the motion of the ball change when you play table tennis?**

table tennis

Stop and Think

1. What is friction?

2. What can happen to an object when the force on it gets stronger?

3. What are some changes in motion?

MORE TO READ

Read **Push and Pull (The Way Things Move)** by Lola M. Schaefer and Gail Saunders-Smith.

Get Ready

This circus boy wants to move the stand. How can he use force to move it? He's got a plan. Can you guess what it is?

Science Skill

You **investigate** when you make a plan and try it out.

Explore Activity

How can force help you lift things?

What you need

book

2 pencils

tape

goggles

What to do  **BE CAREFUL!** Wear goggles.

1. Tape a pencil to your desk. Place the book next to the pencil.

2. Look at the pictures below. Which looks like the easiest way to lift the book?

3. **Investigate** which way is easiest. Make a plan. Then try it out.

4. What was the easiest way to lift the book? Why do you think so?

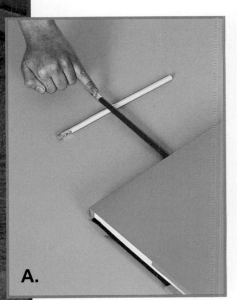
A.

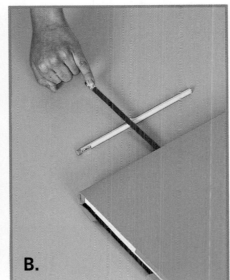
B.

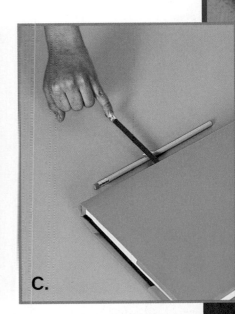
C.

What is a simple machine?

A **simple machine** makes moving an object easier. A simple machine uses force to move the object, or load, from one place to another.

You need to use a lot of force to move a heavy object. When you use a simple machine, you can use less force to move the same object.

▷ **How do you know the seesaw is a simple machine?**

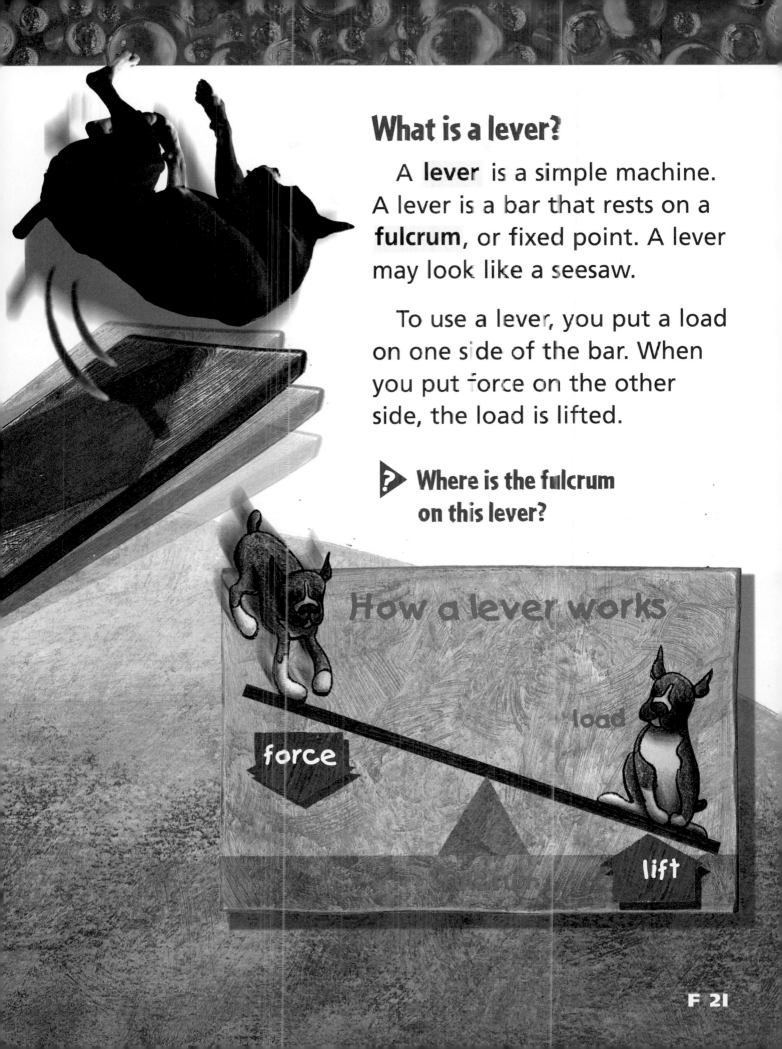

What is a lever?

A **lever** is a simple machine. A lever is a bar that rests on a **fulcrum**, or fixed point. A lever may look like a seesaw.

To use a lever, you put a load on one side of the bar. When you put force on the other side, the load is lifted.

▶ **Where is the fulcrum on this lever?**

How a lever works

force

load

lift

How do we use levers?

You can find levers in many tools. A hand truck is a lever. The fulcrum is the wheel. A pair of scissors is a lever, too. The fulcrum is the point where the blades cross.

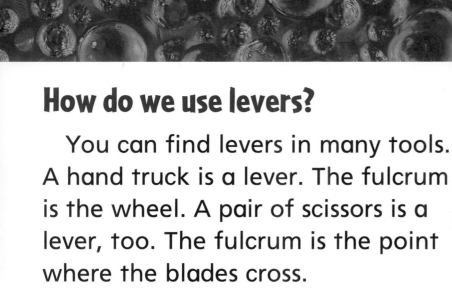

scissors

hand truck

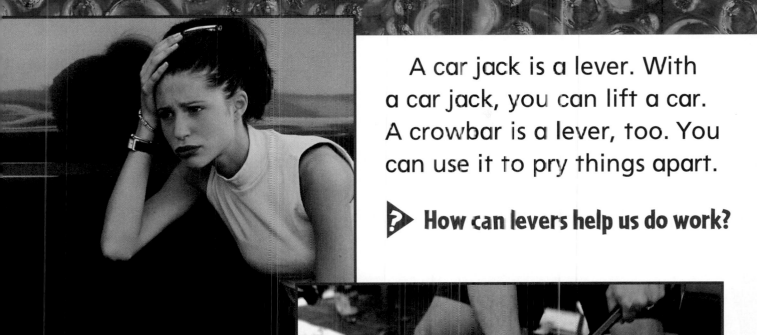

A car jack is a lever. With a car jack, you can lift a car. A crowbar is a lever, too. You can use it to pry things apart.

▷ **How can levers help us do work?**

car jack

crowbar

Stop and Think

1. Why do we use simple machines?

2. Name one kind of simple machine.

3. What tools use levers?

HOME ACTIVITY List any levers you find in your home.

Ramps

Get Ready

Have you ever needed help to lift something? Look at the picture. Would this clown use more or less force if she lifted the elephant on her own? Tell why or why not.

Science Skill

You **measure** something when you find out how much of it there is.

Explore Activity

How can you use less force?

What you need

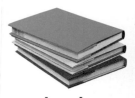

washers

What to do

1 Tie 10 washers onto the end of the string of the Puller Pal.

BE CAREFUL! Wear goggles.

Puller Pal

2 Use the Puller Pal to lift the washers straight up. **Measure** how far the rubber band stretches.

3 Place some books under one end of the board to make a hill. Pull the washers up the board. Measure how far the rubber band stretches.

books

cardboard

4 When was less force needed to move the washers?

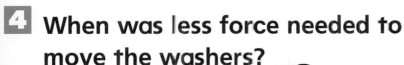

goggles

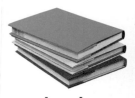

How does a ramp work?

A **ramp** is a simple machine with a slanted surface. A ramp can help you move things to a higher place. It is easier to push a load up a ramp. It takes more force to lift a load without a ramp.

A ramp can be short and steep.
Or it can be longer and less steep.
It takes more force to push
something up a steep ramp than
one that is longer and less steep.

Which ramp makes it easier to push the elephant?

This ramp is longer and less steep!

How do we use ramps?

Ramps help people move objects from one place to another. Many buildings have ramps as well as stairs. They make it easier for people to move from floor to floor.

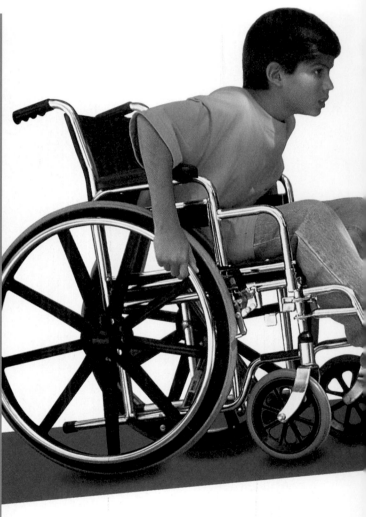

highway ramp

Some ramps are for cars and trucks. Ramps make it possible for these heavy machines to move to high places.

> **How are people in these pictures using ramps?**

boat ramp

loading ramp

wheelchair ramp

Stop and Think

1. What is a ramp?

2. Why is it easier to move something up a ramp than it is to lift it?

3. Name two ways people use ramps.

AT THE COMPUTER Visit **www.mhscience02.com** to find out more about forces and machines.

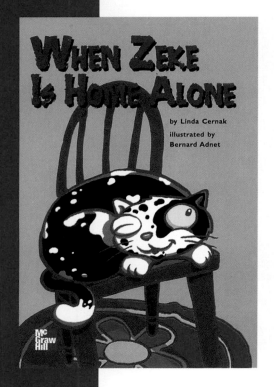

WHEN ZEKE IS HOME ALONE

by Linda Cernak

illustrated by Bernard Adnet

McGraw Hill

Make a Book of Forces

You use pushes and pulls all day long. Find out what everyday activities use force. Read *When Zeke Is Home Alone* by Linda Cernak.

I went down the dide today.

Try This!

Draw pictures of a few ways you use forces during the day. Write a sentence about each. Put your pictures into a book.

Science Newsroom CD-ROM Choose **Gravity** to solve problems about gravity.

Join the Fun Force!

Think about the many different ways you can move. Can you walk in a zigzag line or in a curved line? Can you walk in a straight line or in circles?

Try This!

Play "Follow the Leader" with friends. Take turns being the leader. The leader tells you to move in different ways. As you follow the leader, call out each way you move.

Vocabulary

force

friction

fulcrum

gravity

lever

simple machine

ramp

Use each word once for items 1–7.

1 A push or a pull on an object is a _____ .

2 The force that pulls things toward Earth is _____ .

3 The force that slows down a moving object is _____ .

4 Anything that can change the direction or size of a force is a _____ .

What is the arrow pointing to?

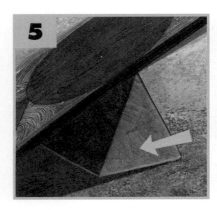

8 If you make a ramp steeper, will it be easier or harder to pull something up it?

9 Which picture does not show a lever?

A

B

C

Science Skill: Observe

10 Which takes more force to move along a table, a ruler or a box of crayons? Use the Puller Pal to find out. Measure how far the rubber band stretches.

Vocabulary

attract

pole

repel

magnetic field

compass

Did You Ever Wonder?

What part of a magnet is the strongest?
This picture shows it. Magnets are
strongest at the ends! Do you know
what kinds of things stick to magnets?

All About Magnets

Get Ready

How do these pins stick without glue? What is holding them on? In what ways are the pins all alike?

Science Skill

You **classify** when you look at how things are alike to put them into groups.

Explore Activity

What will stick to a magnet?

What to do

1 Make a magnet fishing pole. Tie string to a pencil. Tie a magnet to the end of the string.

2 Put all the objects in a bag. Predict which objects will stick to the magnet.

3 Use the fishing pole to fish out objects from the bag.

4 Classify each object to show whether it sticks to the magnet. List the objects on a chart.

Sticks	Does Not Stick

paper bag

small objects

magnet

string

pencil

What does a magnet pull?

A magnet can push and pull. This is called magnetic force.

A magnet can **attract**, or pull, some metals. It attracts metals made of iron. A magnet will not attract things made of copper, brass, plastic, wood, or rubber.

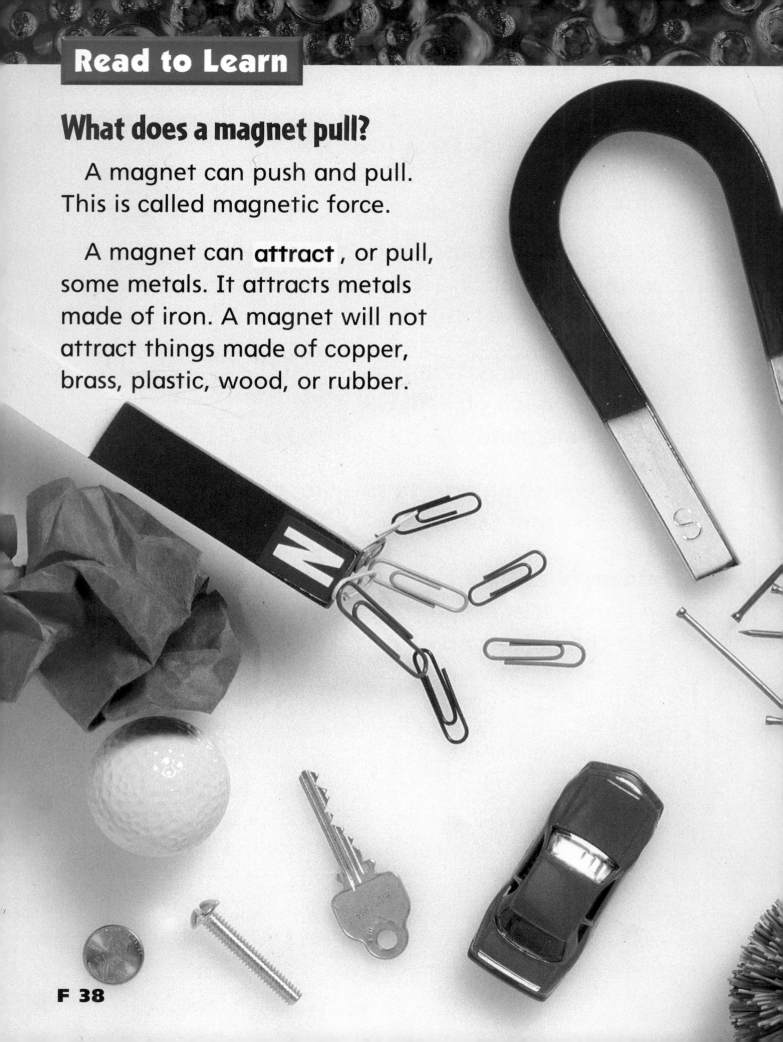

Magnets may have different sizes and shapes. A magnet can be in the shape of a bar, circle, or horseshoe.

Different magnets may also have different pushing and pulling strengths.

▶ **Tell which objects a magnet can attract.**

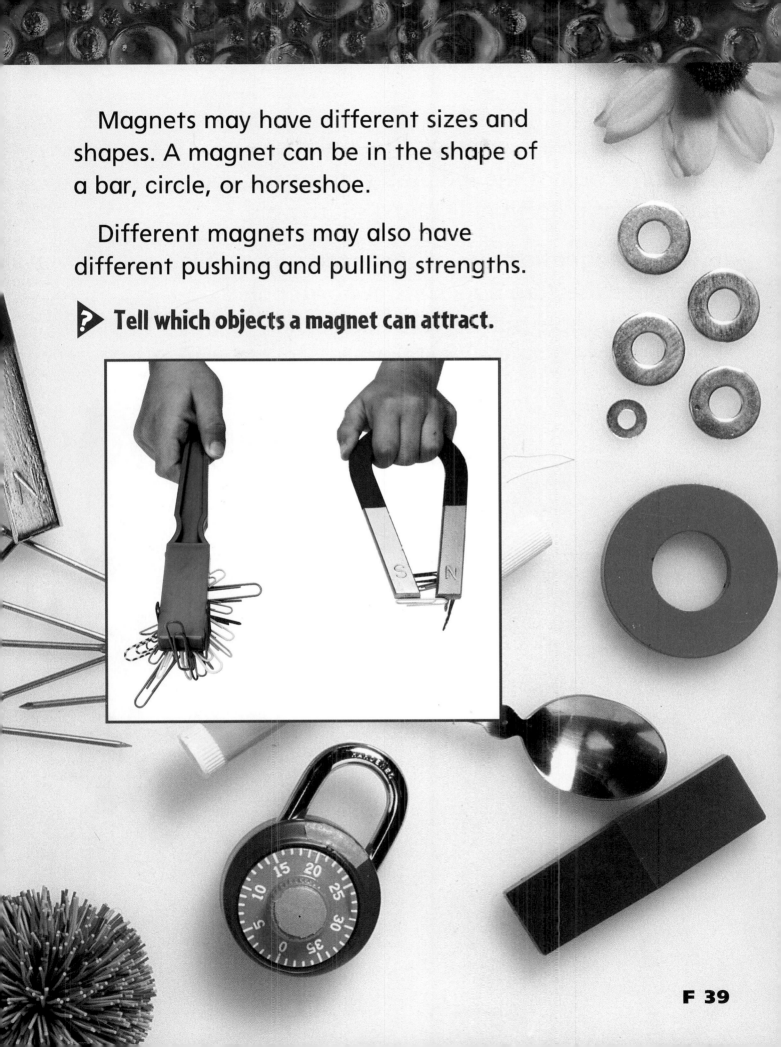

What are poles?

Magnets have two **poles**. The poles are where the pull of the magnet is strongest. Each magnet has a north pole and a south pole.

These magnetic poles attract each other. This is because they are opposites. A north pole and a south pole pull toward each other.

The poles of these magnets **repel**, or push away from, each other. They are repelling each other because they are the same. Two poles that are the same push each other away.

▶ **What would happen if you tried to put two south poles together?**

What can magnets pull through?

Magnets can attract objects without even touching them. The area around a magnet where its force pulls is called a **magnetic field**. A magnetic field can pull through solids, liquids, and gases.

Magnets can pull through liquids.

Magnets can pull through solids.

A magnet's force is strongest when the magnet is close to an iron object. The force grows weaker as the magnet is moved away. When a magnet is moved far enough away from the object, it will not attract the object.

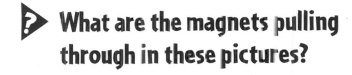

? What are the magnets pulling through in these pictures?

Stop and Think

1. What kinds of objects can magnets attract?

2. What is a magnetic field?

3. Tell what magnets can pull through.

 Read **Magnetism and Magnets** by Michael Flaherty.

LESSON **6**

Everyday Magnets

Get Ready

Look at the picture. What are these kinds of magnets used for? How do they work? If you could make your own magnet, what would you use it for?

Science Skill

You **communicate** when you share your ideas with others.

Explore Activity

How can you make a magnet?

What to do **BE CAREFUL!** Nails are sharp.

1 Stroke the iron nail in one direction on the bar magnet.

2 Lift the nail at the end of each stroke before beginning another. Do this 50 times or more.

3 Test your nail. Can it pick up a paper clip? **Communicate** what happens.

4 What else can your magnet pick up?

What you need

nail

bar magnet

paper clips

can opener

How do we use magnets every day?

You can use a magnet to pick up things or to hold things together. At home, magnets keep your cupboard door closed. Magnets also can lift the top off a can.

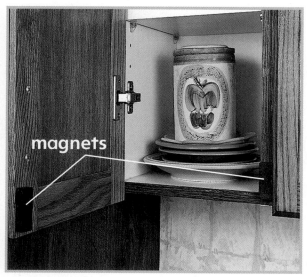

magnets

cupboard door

ITALIAN STYLE
PEELED TOMATOES

screwdriver

Many tools have magnets in them. These tools can make it easier to pick up nails, screws, and bolts.

Some special magnets can help with big jobs. This giant magnet can lift heavy junk from the trash pile.

 How are these magnets being used?

How else do we use Earth's magnetic field?

Did you know that Earth is like a giant magnet? It has a North Pole and a South Pole. Earth's magnetic field stretches out into space. Like all magnets, Earth's pulling force is strongest at its poles.

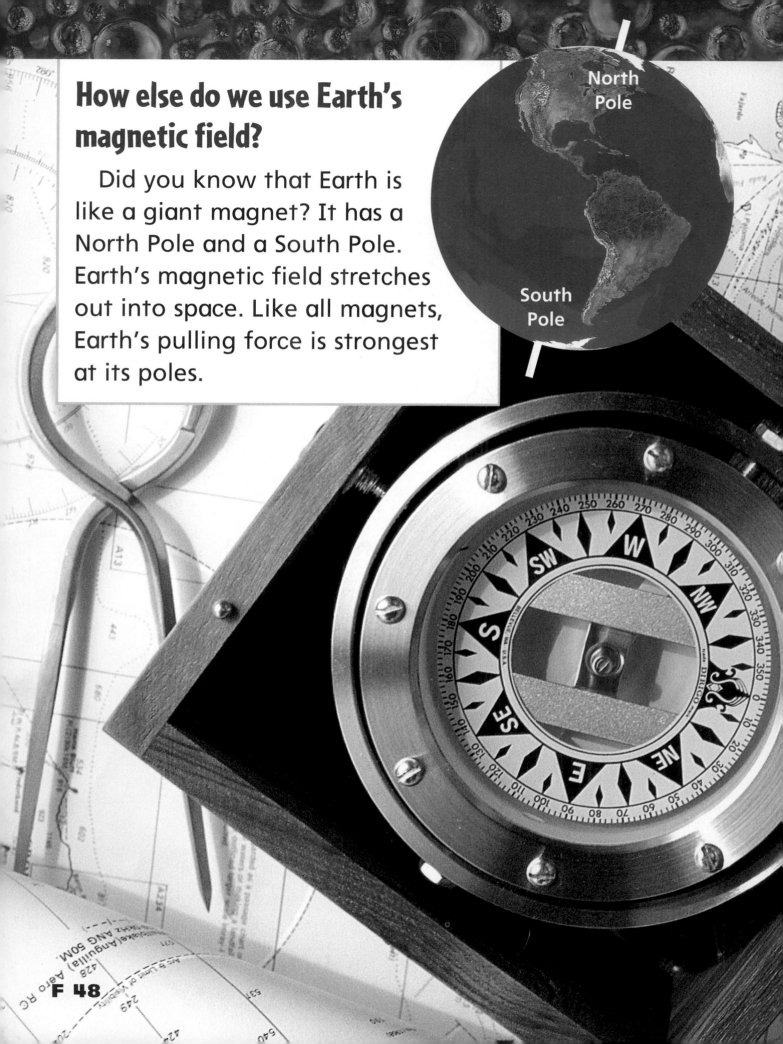

North Pole

South Pole

People use Earth's magnetic field to help them find their way. A **compass** is a tool with a magnetic needle that always points to Earth's North Pole. With a compass, you can always figure out which direction you are facing.

▷ **What is a compass needle attracted to?**

Stop and Think

1. What are some ways we use magnets?

2. Where is Earth's magnetic field the strongest?

3. What is a compass?

HOME ACTIVITY Go on a magnet hunt at home. List each magnet you find. Tell how it is used.

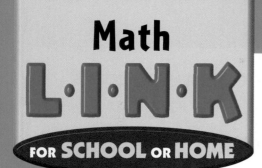
Test a Magnet's Strength

Some magnets are stronger than others. You can compare their strengths by testing how much each one attracts.

Try This!

Hang a line of paper clips from different magnets until no more will hang on. Count how many clips each magnet holds. Record your findings on a bar graph.

Make Your Own Compass

Many people use compasses to help them find their way. You can, too.

Try This!

Have an adult help you make your own magnet like you did in the Explore Activity. Magnetize a large, straightened paper clip. Stick the paper clip through a foam ball or a cork. Float it in a big bowl of water. Wait until it stops moving. Which way is north?

Vocabulary

attract

compass

magnetic field

poles

repel

Use each word once for items I–5.

1 The strongest parts of a magnet are its ____ .

2 The area around a magnet where the force works is called a ____ .

3 Opposite poles of a magnet pull, or ____ .

4 The same poles of two magnets ____ each other.

5 A tool with a magnetic needle that always points to Earth's North Pole is a ____ .

Science Ideas

6 Which of the following will a magnet pick up?

A

B

C

7 Where is the force of a magnet strongest?

8 What would happen if the north poles of two magnets were placed near each other? Why?

Science Skill: Investigate

9 Make a plan to figure out which magnet below would hold the most pieces of paper to a refrigerator. Write the plan. Get what you need to test your plan. Then try it out.

READ
Ride a Floating Train by Richie Chevat

Rube Goldberg

Artist

Rube Goldberg was a cartoon artist. So what does that have to do with science? He was also an engineer. Rube drew cartoons that showed complicated machines. Each machine did a simple job, such as closing a window. His machines are funny.

Today many schools hold Rube Goldberg contests. To compete, students build real machines that do simple jobs. Each machine must go through 20 or more steps to complete the job.

 Invent a wacky machine to do something. Draw and write your ideas.

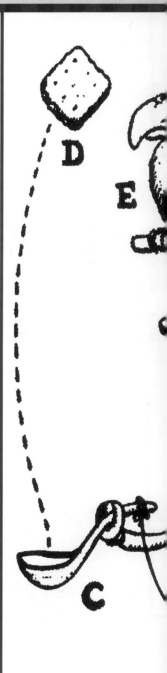

This cartoon is called "Self-operating Napkin." The machine uses a parrot, a lighter, a rocket, a clock, and other gadgets – all to wipe soup off of a person's chin!

AT THE COMPUTER

Visit **www.mhscience02.com** to find out more about Rube Goldberg.

SCIENCE
Workshop

1. Forces in Sports Choose a sport that you like. Draw a picture of you or a friend playing it. Write or tell how you use each of these things while playing:

- push or pull

- gravity

- friction

2. Magnet Hunt Go on a magnet hunt around your home or school. Choose one magnet and write about it. How is the magnet used? What does it attract? How strong is its pulling force? How can you test it out?

Exploring Virginia

The Northern Cardinal is
the Virginia state bird.

Soybeans

Lightning

Charlottesville

James River

Roanoke

VIRGI

Roanoke River

ST
INIA

UCKY

Abingdon

Raccoon

Northern
Cardinal

CAROLI

Exploring Virginia

LIFE SCIENCE

EARTH SCIENCE

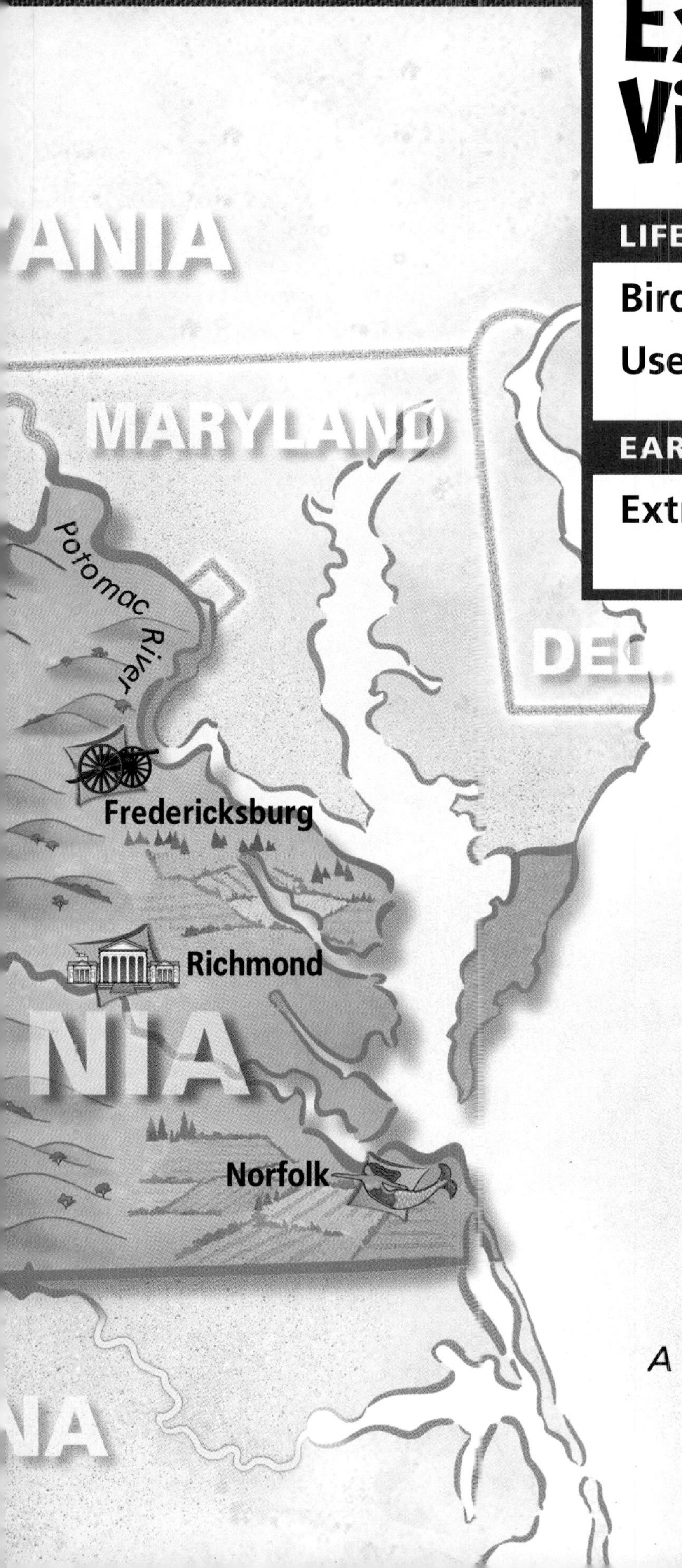

ANIA
MARYLAND
Potomac River
DEL
Fredericksburg
Richmond
NIA
Norfolk
NA
Atlantic
Ocean

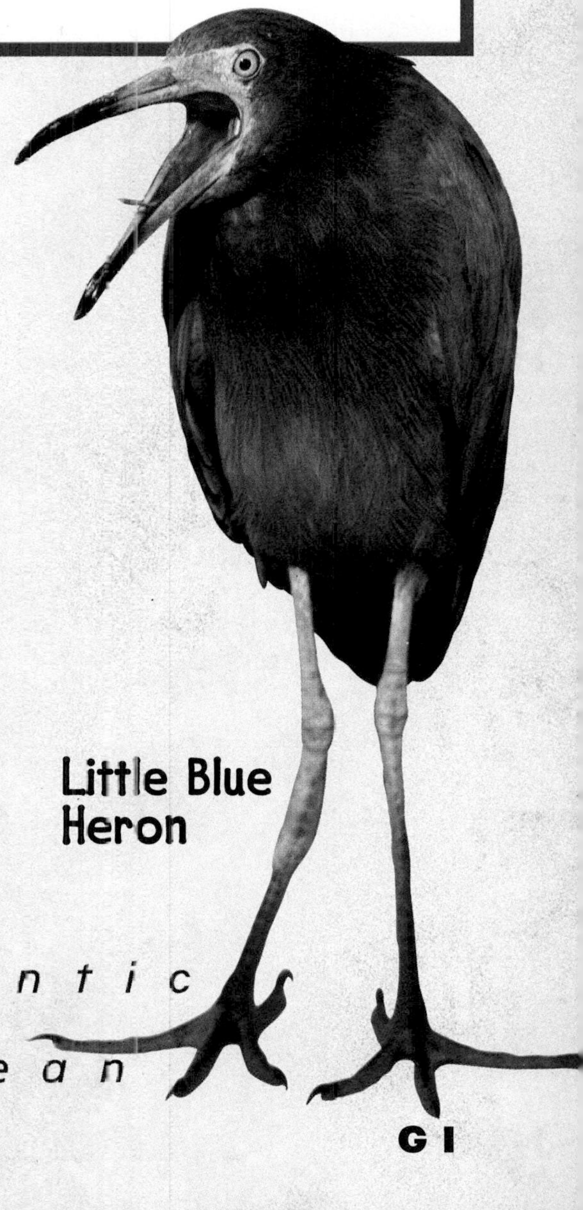

Little Blue Heron

Our Feathered Friends

What do you need to watch birds? Be patient and use your eyes and ears.

Be quiet and sit still. You will see and hear many birds.

Northern Mockingbird

ACTIVITY

■ Binoculars help you get a closer look at birds. Practice using a pair of binoculars. Ask an adult for help.

■ Field guides help you identify the kinds of birds you see. Spend some time looking at bird field guides.

Start looking and listening for birds wherever you go. Notice birds at home and in your schoolyard.

Mourning Dove

First, learn to identify the birds you see most often. Some birds you can see are jays, crows, and robins.

Blue Jay

ACTIVITY

- Which kinds of birds will you see in one-half hour?

- Draw pictures of the birds you see. Learn their names.

- Did you see birds you thought you would? Did you see birds that you didn't think you would?

- Do the activity on 2 other days. Did you see the same kinds of birds?

Northern Cardinal

How can we identify birds?

Birds can be different colors, shapes, and sizes. Is the bird plump or thin, tall or short?

Swamp Canary

Does the bird have long, pointed wings or short, rounded wings? Look for wingbars.

American Goldfinch

Does it have a crest or special colors or stripes on its head? Is there a ring around its eye?

Beaks can be long or short, thin or thick.

Brown Pelican

The tail can be short or long. Is it pointy or forked? Is it round tipped or square tipped?

Does the bird have stripes or spots on its breast? Does it have patches of color on its throat, wings, or rump?

Eastern Bluebird

Wild Turkey

Does it have webbed feet for swimming or talons for holding prey? Does it have long or short legs?

Mallard

ACTIVITY

Use a hand lens to look at feathers. Can you see different colors? Are they from the wings, tail, or body? What bird are they from?

How do birds fly?

Different birds use their wings to fly in different ways.

The Hummingbird hovers in one spot.

A Bald Eagle can soar.

An Egret's long legs follow behind as the bird beats its wings.

What do birds eat?

Barn Owl

Downy
Woodpecker

Birds eat seeds, fruit, insects, and
other animals. Some birds catch and
eat other birds and mammals. Others
eat dead animals.

Cedar
Waxwing
family

ACTIVITY

- Put different types of
  seeds and fruit in
  containers for birds.

- Record which birds are
  eating which foods.

- Compare beak shape
  and size with food
  items eaten.

G 7

Where do birds live?

Each kind of bird has its favorite place to live. Some live in forests, and others live in meadows and fields.

Chimney Swifts

Chimney Swifts build nests in chimneys and are fun to watch! In cities, look for starlings, pigeons, and House Finches.

Virginia Rail

Birds can nest in trees or near rivers and marshes. The Virginia Rail lays her eggs near a marsh.

Starlings

Do all birds sound alike?

Every kind of bird has its own song and calls. You can learn to identify birds by their voices.

The same kind of bird can look and sound different when it lives in different places. Birds have accents just like us.

Little Blue Herons make croaking sounds.

TAKING CARE OF Birds

- It is fun to watch birds. Treat them with care and respect. Look at, but don't touch, nests, eggs, or young birds.

- Be still and watch birds from a distance. They will keep doing what they are doing. You will get to watch them longer.

ACTIVITY

- Learn the songs of five common birds. Use a tape recording of birdsongs. Your teacher will help you.

G 9

Useful Plants from Around the World

Plants grow all around the world. Plants are grown to make things people use.

United States

South America

Much of the lumber and paper we use come from trees that grow in the Pacific Northwest.

People use red peppers for cooking. South America is one place where they grow.

India and China are places where cotton plants grow. Cotton is used for clothing and for many other things.

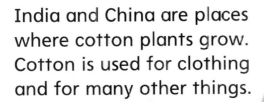

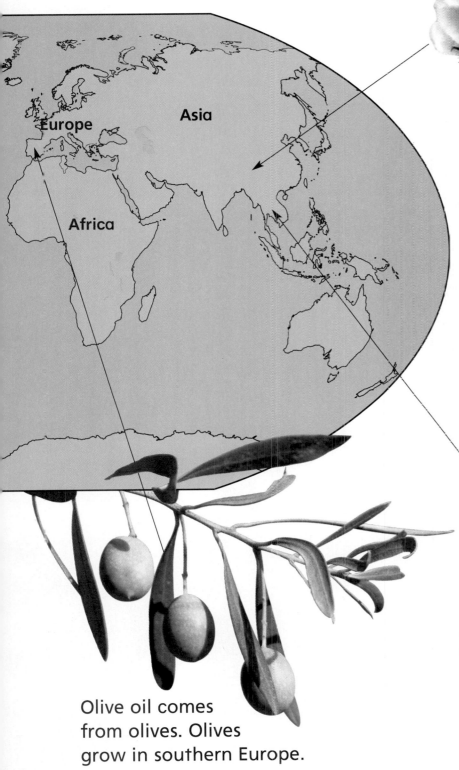

Rubber trees that grow in southeast Asia are used to make boots and other rubber items.

Olive oil comes from olives. Olives grow in southern Europe.

Useful Plants from Virginia

Most crops in Virginia are grown on family farms. Here are a few of the many crops grown in Virginia.

Grain corn

Soybean crop

Soybeans

It takes a lot of land to grow crops. That's why farmland is not like the land in cities.

Cotton

Peanuts

Extreme Weather

Rain and sunhine are important to living things. But some kinds of weather can be dangerous. When storms come, you should seek shelter—a place that is safe from the storm.

In a thunderstorm, lightning may strike a tree and start a fire.

Some storms bring funnels of wind called tornadoes. A tornado can destroy everything in its path.

A hurricane can blow down trees and buildings. Its floodwaters can wash away cars and homes.

Drought happens when there is no rain for a long time. Drought destroys crops.

ACTIVITY

■ Make a list of things you should NOT do in a thunderstorm. Tell why.

Glossary

C crops plants grown for use by people (page G 12)
Soybeans, corn, and cotton are some crops grown in Virginia.

D drought a long period without rain (page G 15)
Drought destroys crops.

H hurricane a powerful storm that causes flooding and damage (page G 15)
A hurricane brings strong winds and flooding

T thunderstorm a kind of weather that includes rain, lightning, thunder, and sometimes hail (page G 14).
Stay indoors during a thunderstorm.

tornado a funnel of wind that destroys everything in its path (page G 15)
Seek shelter during a tornado.

Illustrations: Karen Minot: p. G1.

Photography Credits:
All photographs are by Macmillan/McGraw-Hill (MMH) except as noted below:

Unit Opener: Bill Goulet/Bruce Coleman, Inc./PictureQuest.

Contents: G1: b.l.l. Gary W. Carter/Corbis; b.l.r. Steven W. Jones/FPG International; b.r. Zig Leszczynski/Animals Animals; t.l.l. PhotoDisc; t.l.r. Corbis.

Unit G: G2: bkgrd Ed Reschke/Peter Arnold, Inc.; inset Ed Reschke/Peter Arnold, Inc. G3: b.l. Gary W Carter/Corbis; m.l. Tom Vezo/Peter Arnold, Inc.; t.r. Russell C. Hansen/Peter Arnold, Inc. G4: b. Ted & Jean Reuther/Dembinsky Photo Associates; m.l. Wayne Lankinen/DRK Photo; t. inset John Snyder/Bruce Coleman, Inc. G5: m. Rick & Nora Bowers/Visuals Unlimited, Inc.; r. Dick Scott/Visuals Unlimited, Inc.; t.l.

Adam Jones/Photo Researchers, Inc. G6: b. Phyllis Greenberg/Animals Animals; m. Johnny Johnson/DRK Photo; t.r. Charles Melton/Visuals Unlimited, Inc. G7: b. Gregory K. Scott/Photo Researchers, Inc.; t.l. Gerard Lacz/Peter Arnold, Inc.; t.r. Joe McDonald/Visuals Unlimited, Inc. G8: b.r. Paul B. Swarmer/Visuals Unlimited, Inc.; l. Tim Zurowski/Corbis; t.r. Richard & Susan Day/Animals Animals. G9: b. Joe McDonald/Visuals Unlimited, Inc.; t. Zig Leszczynski/Animals Animals. G10: b.r. Patrick Johns/Corbis; l. Kevin Fleming/Corbis; m. Steffan Widstrand/Corbis. G11: b.l. Wolfgang Kaehler/Corbis; b.r. Macduff Everton/Corbis; t.r. Lance Nelson/Corbis. G12: bkgrd Richard Hamilton-Smith/Corbis; l. Phillip Gould/Corbis; r. PhotoDisc. G13: m. Lance Nelson/Corbis; r. Michael Barley/Corbis. G14: bkgrd Corbis; l. inset Erwin & Peggy Bauer/Bruce Coleman, Inc.; r. inset Erwin & Peggy Bauer/Bruce Coleman, Inc. G15: l. Art Wolfe/Getty Images; r. Corbis; t. Paul & Linda Marie Ambrose/Getty Images.

For Your Reference

Skills Handbook

Science Handbook

Health Handbook

Glossary

Science Skill Builder 1

Observe

Your senses help you **observe** things. How? Your senses tell you how things look, sound, feel, smell, or taste.

What to do

1 Observe something in the Science Center.

2 How does it look? Feel? Smell? Sound?

3 Draw and write about it.

4 What object did you observe? Which of your senses helped you the most?

What you need

pencil

crayons

paper

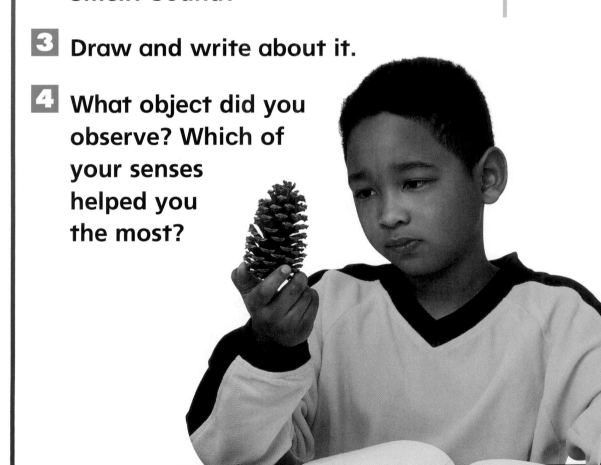

Science Skill Builder 2

Measure

You can **measure** to find out how long, how fast, or how warm something is. You use numbers to record the answer.

What you need

2 cups
of water

2
thermometers

What to do

1 Fill one cup with warm water. Fill the other cup with cold water.

2 Place a thermometer in each cup. Wait 2 minutes.

3 Record each temperature.

4 What other things can you **measure** with a thermometer?

Science Skill Builder 3

Compare

You observe things to **compare** them. You find out how they are alike and different.

What you need

paper

pencil

What to do

1 **Compare** the second graders in the picture.

2 List three ways they are alike.

3 List three ways they are different.

Science Skill Builder 4

Classify

You **classify** when you make groups that are alike in some way.

What you need

paper

pencil

What to do

1 Look at the picture of the beans.

2 Classify the beans by size. Draw the two groups. Label them Big and Small.

3 Find another way to classify the beans. Write labels for the new groups.

Make a Model

You **make a model** when you do something to show a place or thing. A model can help you learn how a place looks or how a thing works.

What to do

1 **Make a model** of a clock. Include numbers and hands.

BE CAREFUL! Scissors are sharp.

2 What can you learn about a real clock from the model?

3 How is the real thing different from the model?

What you need

paper

crayons

scissors

paper fastener

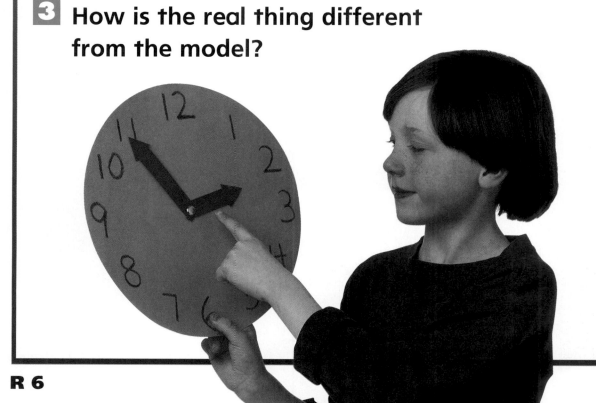

Science Skill Builder 6

Communicate

You **communicate** to share your ideas. You can talk, write, or draw to communicate.

What you need

paper

pencil

What to do

1 Think about your favorite food.

2 Write a description of that food.

3 **Communicate** to a friend. Read your description. Ask your friend to name the food you described.

Science Skill Builder 7

Infer

To **infer**, you use what you know to figure something out.

What to do

1 Look at the pictures.

2 Use what you know to **infer** which place is warmer.

3 Write a short story to tell what games children can play in each place.

What you need

paper

pencil

Put Things in Order

To put things **in order**, you tell what happens first, next, and last.

What to do

1 Think about all the things that you did after you woke up this morning.

2 List each thing on your paper. Write them **in order**.

3 Draw a picture of you doing one of those things.

What you need

pencil

crayons

paper

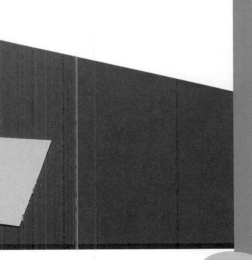

Predict

You use what you already know to help you **predict** what will happen next.

"I'm hungry," said Laura.

"Me, too," replied Jack.

"I wish I had a snack," Laura said.

"All I have are these grapes," said Jack.

What you need

crayons

paper

What to do

1 Read the story above.

2 **Predict** what you think will happen next.

3 Draw a picture to show it.

Science Skill Builder 10

Investigate

To **investigate**, you make a plan and try it out.

What you need

pencils

clay

blocks

What to do

1 **Investigate** a plan for building a clay and pencil shape. It should be able to hold up at least 2 small blocks.

2 Try it out.

3 Place as many blocks as you can on your shape. How many did it hold before it fell?

Draw a Conclusion

To draw a **conclusion**, you use what you observe to explain what happens.

What to do

1 Look at the picture. Where do you think the girl is going? What will she do there?

2 Draw a conclusion. Show it in a picture.

crayons

paper

Save and Recycle

We should not waste things.

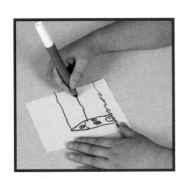

**Use no more
than you need.**

**Don't leave
the water on.**

**Recycle as much
as you can.**

**Use things more
than once.**

Care of Animals

Here are ways to care for animals.

- Give pets food and water. Give them a safe place to live, too.

- Be kind to pets. Handle them with care.

- Don't touch wild animals. They may bite, sting, or scratch you.

- Do not touch things in places where wild animals live.

Care of Plants

Here are ways to care for plants.

- Give plants water and sunlight.

- Ask the teacher before you touch or eat a plant. Some plants can make you very sick!

- Do not dig up plants or pick flowers. Let plants grow where they are.

Clean Up

We need to keep work places clean.

Let an adult clean up broken glass.

Pour water into a sink, not into a trash can.

Put food in plastic bags. This keeps bugs away.

Don't get paint or food on you.

How to Measure

You can use many things to measure.

This string is about 8 paper clips long.

This string is about 3 pencils long.

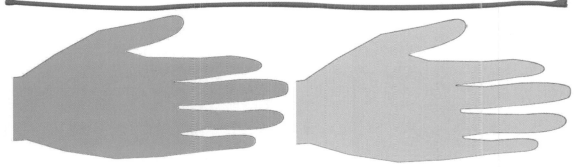

This string is about 2 hands long.

Try This!

- Measure some string. Tell how you did it.

- Can you measure string with these paper clips? Why or why not?

Units of Measurement

There are other ways to measure. You can use centimeters (cm) or meters (m). These are called units of measurement.

The crayon is about 8 centimeters long. We write this as 8 cm.

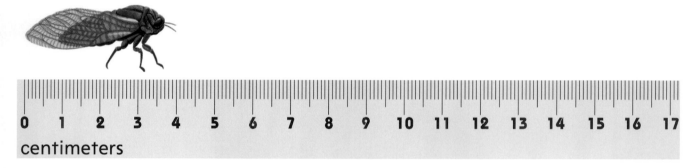

The insect is about 4 centimeters long. We write this as 4 cm.

• How long is this pencil?

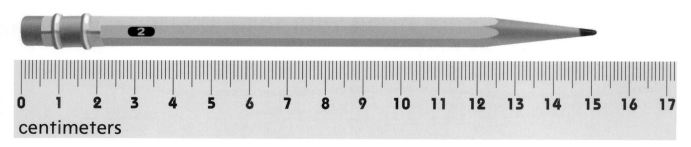

Use a Ruler

0 1 2 3 4 5 6 7 8 9 10 11 12 13 14 15 16
centimeters

You can use a ruler to measure this leaf.
Line up the end of the leaf with the 0
on the ruler. The leaf is about 11
centimeters, or 11 cm.

Try This!

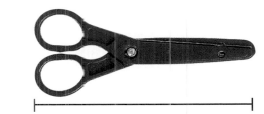

Estimate how long
each object is. Use
a ruler to measure.

Object	Estimate	Measure
scissors	about ____ cm	about ____ cm
penny	about ____ cm	about ____ cm
toy car	about ____ cm	about ____ cm

Use a Thermometer

A thermometer measures temperature.

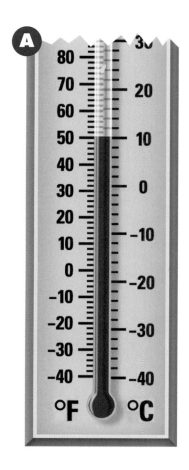

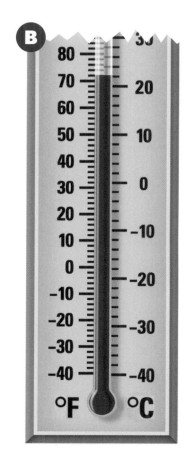

It gets warmer. The liquid in a thermometer moves up.

It gets cooler. The liquid in a thermometer moves down.

Which thermometer shows a warmer temperature? How can you tell?

A thermometer has marks with numbers.

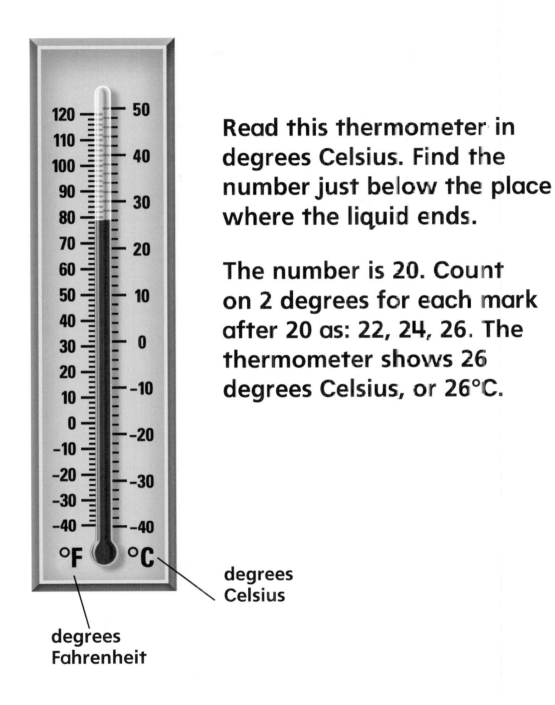

degrees
Celsius

degrees
Fahrenheit

Read this thermometer in degrees Celsius. Find the number just below the place where the liquid ends.

The number is 20. Count on 2 degrees for each mark after 20 as: 22, 24, 26. The thermometer shows 26 degrees Celsius, or 26°C.

What temperatures are shown on page R20?

Use a Measuring Cup

Volume is the amount of space something takes up. You can use a measuring cup to find volume.

The marks on this cup show the number of milliliters. There are 500 milliliters (500 mL) of water in this cup.

measuring cup

Try This!

- Get 3 different small containers.

- Which holds the most? Which holds the least?

- Fill each container with water. Pour the water into the measuring cup. Find the volumes.

Use a Balance

A balance compares mass.

Place one object on each side of the balance. The object that has more mass will make that side of the balance go down. The object that has less mass will make that side of the balance go up.

Try This!

- Place 2 objects on a balance. Which has more mass?

- Put 3 objects in order from least mass to most mass. Use the balance to check.

Before you compare mass, make sure the arrow points to the line.

Use a Clock

A clock measures time.

Each mark means
1 minute.

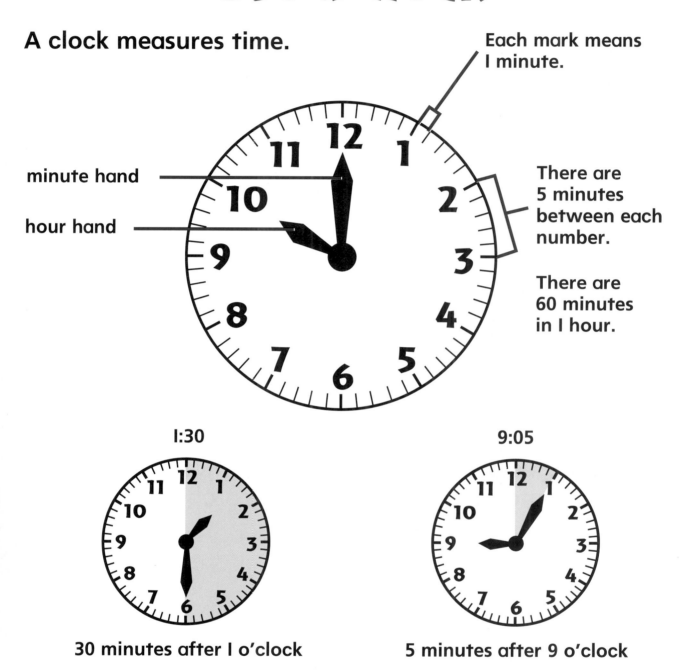

minute hand

hour hand

There are
5 minutes
between each
number.

There are
60 minutes
in 1 hour.

1:30

30 minutes after 1 o'clock

9:05

5 minutes after 9 o'clock

Try This!

How long do you think it takes to write your
name 5 times? Have a friend time you.

Use a Hand Lens

A hand lens makes objects seems larger.

First, move the lens away from the object. Stop when the object looks fuzzy.

Next, move the lens a little closer to the object. Stop when the object looks clear.

Try This!

- Observe each bug here. Use a hand lens.

- How many legs do you see on the bugs?

- What else can you see?

R 25

Use a Computer

A computer is a tool that can get information.

You can use CD-ROMs. They have a lot of information. You can fit many books on one CD-ROM!

You can also use the Internet. The Internet links your computer to ones far away.

Try This!

- Use the Internet. Visit **www.mhscience02.com** and learn more about science in your world.

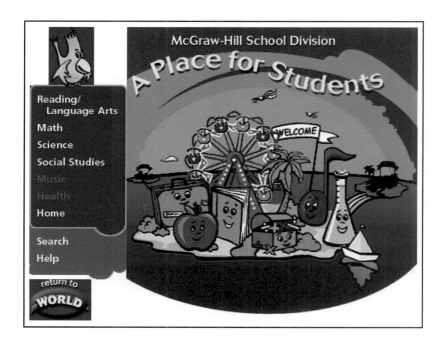

McGraw-Hill School Division

A Place for Students

Reading/Language Arts
Math
Science
Social Studies
Music
Health
Home

Search
Help

return to WORLD

WELCOME

Your Body Parts

Each part of your body has a job to do.

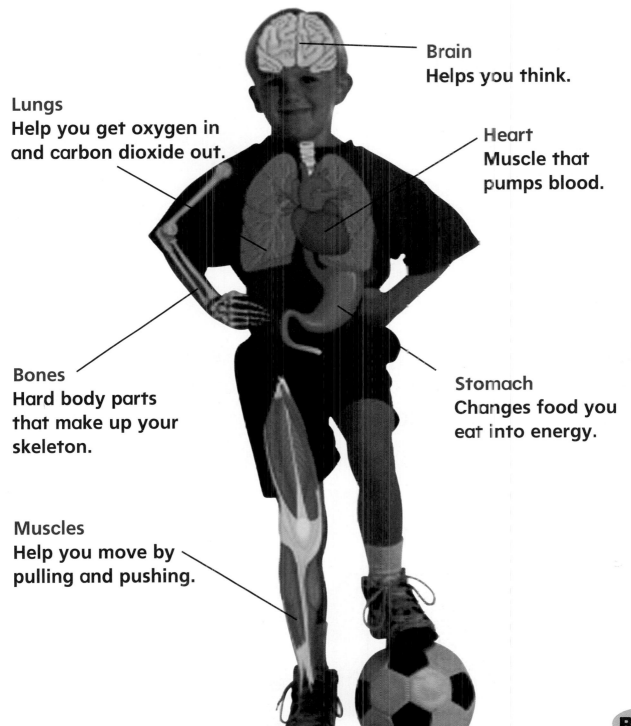

Brain
Helps you think.

Lungs
Help you get oxygen in and carbon dioxide out.

Heart
Muscle that pumps blood.

Bones
Hard body parts that make up your skeleton.

Stomach
Changes food you eat into energy.

Muscles
Help you move by pulling and pushing.

Look Your Best

Keep your body neat and clean.

Brush and floss your teeth.

Take care of your hair and nails.

Stand, sit up, and walk with your back straight.

Be Active and Rest

Be active every day.

Get plenty of sleep at night.

Your body needs both to help you grow!

Eat Healthful Foods

Choose healthful foods.

Healthful foods give
your body energy.

Milk and fruit are healthful foods.

So are bread and vegetables.

Healthful foods help you grow
and stay well.

Getting Along

Work and play well with others.

In many ways you are alike, but in some ways you may be different. Respect one another's feelings.

Show others that you care.

Be Safe Indoors

Some things are dangerous. Don't touch them!
Tell an adult when you find something dangerous.

Be Safe Outdoors

Stay Healthy

Your body grows and changes.

Get a checkup every year.

Find out how much you've grown and changed!

Glossary

A

amphibians animals that start their lives in the water *(page A35)* **Frogs and toads are amphibians.**

Arctic a very cold place near the North Pole *(page B24)* **In the Arctic, snow is on the ground for much of the year.**

attract to pull *(page F38)* **A magnet can attract some metals.**

axis a line through the center of a spinning object *(page D6)* **Earth's axis is an imaginary line that goes from the North Pole to the South Pole.**

axis

C

chemical change a change in matter that makes new matter *(page E22)* **When metal rusts, it is a chemical change.**

classify to put things into groups to show how they are alike *(page A4)* **You can classify things into groups.**

legs

no legs

AT THE COMPUTER

Visit **www.mhscience02.com** to find out more about these words.

communicate to share your ideas with others *(page A36)* **Scientists communicate to learn and to show what they know.**

compare to tell how things are alike and different *(page D10)* **You can compare how two objects are alike.**

compass a tool with a magnetic needle that always points to Earth's North Pole *(page F49)* **With a compass, you can figure out which direction you are facing.**

condense to change into liquid *(page C7)* **Cool air makes water vapor condense.**

constellation a star pattern that makes a picture *(page D40)* **The Big Dipper and the Little Dipper are constellations.**

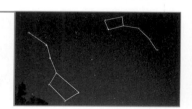

craters large holes on the surface of the Moon *(page D27)* **Many Moon craters were made by rocks falling from space.**

D

desert a dry habitat that gets very little rainfall *(page B20)* **A desert gets less than ten inches of rain each year.**

draw a conclusion use what you observe to explain what happens *(page B18)* **You can draw a conclusion about what kind of weather is shown here.**

E

earthquake a shaking of the ground caused by a shift of Earth's crust *(page C20)* **An earthquake causes Earth to change.**

endangered in danger of becoming extinct *(page C48)* **The giant panda is an endangered animal.**

energy the power to make matter move or change *(page E32)* **Fireworks make light, heat, and sound energy.**

equator the imaginary line across the middle of Earth that separates the northern part from the southern part *(page D16)* **The United States is north of the equator.**

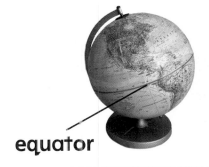

equator

erosion when worn down rocks are carried away *(page C14)* **The Grand Canyon was caused by erosion.**

evaporate to change into gas *(page C6)* **As the boy's sweatshirt dries, the water will evaporate.**

extinct when a thing dies out and no more of its kind are living anywhere on Earth *(page C46)* **The woolly mammoth is extinct.**

F

flower the part of a plant that makes seeds *(page A12)* **Seeds grow inside the flower.**

food chain the order in which living things need each other for food *(page A41)* **In a food chain, each animal uses another living thing as food.**

food web a group of several food chains that are connected *(page B42)* **Plankton is an important part of the ocean food web.**

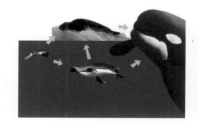

force a push or a pull that makes something move or change direction *(page F6)* **The force of a push helps the girl move forward.**

fossils what is left of living things from the past *(page C32)* **Some fossils are animal footprints.**

friction a force that slows down moving things *(page F12)* **A skater stops by using friction.**

fruit the part of a plant that grows around seeds *(page A13)* **The fruit protects the seeds.**

fuel something that gives off heat when it burns *(page E34)* **Wood, natural gas, and oil are fuels.**

fulcrum the fixed point on which a lever rests *(page F21)* **A seesaw rests on a fulcrum.**

G

gas a state of matter that spreads out to fill its container *(page E16)* **A balloon is filled with gas.**

gravity a force that pulls things toward Earth *(page F7)* **Gravity pulls the sled down the hill.**

H

habitat a place where plants and animals can meet their needs *(page B6)* **The plants and animals in a habitat need each other in many ways.**

heat a kind of energy that can make something melt or boil *(page E32)* **Heat can change the state of matter.**

I

infer use what you know to figure something out *(page A14)* **You may be able to infer what kind of animal made these footprints.**

investigate make a plan and try it out *(page E18)* **You can investigate how to make a magnet attract a paper clip through water.**

L

landslide a sudden movement of soil down a hill *(page C21)* **A landslide can destroy homes.**

larva the stage in the life cycle of a butterfly when the insect is a caterpillar *(page A48)* **A caterpillar is a larva.**

lever a simple machine made of a bar that rests on a fixed point *(page F21)* **You can make a lever with two pencils.**

life cycle shows how a living thing grows, lives, and dies *(page A18)* **A bear's life cycle shows how a bear grows.**

light a kind of energy that lets us see *(page E38)* **We use electric light to help us see indoors.**

liquid a state of matter that takes the shape of its container *(page E14)* **Juice is a liquid.**

M

magnetic field the area around a magnet where its force pulls *(page F42)* **A magnetic field can pull through solids, liquids, and gases.**

make a model make something to show a place or thing *(page B8)* **You can make a model to show where leaf bats live.**

mammals animals with hair or fur that breathe with body parts called lungs *(page A34)* **Female mammals make milk for their babies.**

mass the amount of matter in an object (*page E7*) **A feather has less mass than a crayon.**

matter anything that takes up space and has mass (*page E6*) **Everything in this fish tank is made of matter.**

measure find out how long, how much, or how warm something is (*page F4*) **You can measure to find out which of these items is longer.**

migrate to move to another place (*page B13*) **In winter these animals migrate from the Arctic to a warmer habitat.**

minerals bits of rock and soil that break down (*page A7*) **Plants use minerals in the soil to stay healthy.**

Moon a ball of rock that orbits around Earth (*page D26*) **It takes the Moon $29\frac{1}{2}$ days to orbit Earth.**

O

observe to use your senses to learn about the world around you (*page B38*) **Scientists observe things to learn more about them.**

ocean a large, deep body of salt water *(page B40)* **Dolphins live in the ocean.**

orbit the path an object takes as it moves around another object *(page D12)* **The Moon orbits Earth.**

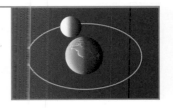

order show what happens first, second, third, and last *(page A44)* **When you put things in order you can tell what will happen next.**

oxygen a gas made by plants that is found in the air we breathe *(page A23)* **A whale needs to breathe oxygen to live.**

P

paleontologist a scientist who studies things that lived long ago *(page C38)* **A paleontologist finds and studies fossils.**

phase a change in the Moon's shape as we can see from Earth *(page D32)* **We see phases of the Moon because we see different parts of its lit side.**

physical change to change the size or shape of matter *(page E20)* **Cutting food is a physical change.**

pitch how high or how low a sound is *(page E47)* **A xylophone goes from a high pitch to a low pitch.**

planet a huge object that travels around the Sun *(page D44)* **Saturn is a planet in our solar system.**

poles the ends of a magnet where the pull is strongest *(page F40)* **Every magnet has two poles.**

pollen the powder inside a flower that can make seeds grow *(page A16)* **The bee carries the pollen from flower to flower.**

pollution waste that harms land, water, or air *(page B46)* **Pollution hurts both living and nonliving things.**

pond a fresh water habitat in which the water stays in one place *(page B34)* **Beavers build their homes in a pond.**

precipitation water falling from the sky as rain, snow, and hail *(page C9)* **Rain is a kind of precipitation.**

predator an animal that hunts another animal for food *(page A40)* **Sharks are predators.**

predict use what you know to tell what will happen *(page A10)* **You can predict what might grow from these seeds.**

prey an animal that is being hunted *(page A40)* **The bird is the cat's prey.**

property tells you something about an object *(page E8)* **Big, brown, and fuzzy are all properties of this bear.**

pupa the stage in the life cycle of a butterfly when a caterpillar spins a hard case around itself *(page A48)* **Inside the hard case, the pupa changes into a butterfly.**

R

rain forest a habitat that gets rain almost every day *(page B16)* **A rain forest can get more than 70 inches of rain each year.**

ramp a simple machine with a slanted surface *(page F26)* **A ramp makes it easier to move from place to place.**

recycle use waste to make new things that can be used again *(page B49)* **We can recycle paper, glass, cans, and plastic.**

reflects when light bounces off an object *(page E38)* **A mirror reflects light.**

refraction when something bends light *(page E39)* **Refraction can make something look bigger.**

repel to push away from *(page F41)* **The poles of these magnets repel each other.**

reptiles animals with dry, scaly skin *(page A34)* **Snakes are reptiles.**

rotates spins *(page D6)* **Earth rotates on its axis.**

rotates——

S

seeds the plant parts that can grow into new plants *(page A13)* **When seeds get water, warmth, and air, they begin to grow.**

shelter a place where an animal can live and be safe *(page A42)* **Foxes find shelter in a hole.**

simple machine something that changes the direction or size of force to make work easier *(page F20)* **Hand trucks and ramps are simple machines.**

skeleton a full set of bones *(page C39)* **A dinosaur skeleton helps scientists learn more about what they looked like.**

solar system the Sun, nine planets, and all of their moons *(page D44)* **The Sun is the center of our solar system.**

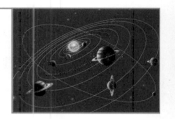

solid a state of matter that has a shape of its own *(page E12)* **This wooden block is a solid.**

sound a kind of energy that you hear *(page E44)* **When you crash cymbals together, they make a loud sound.**

star a hot ball in the sky that makes its own light *(page D38)* **A star looks tiny because it is so far away from Earth.**

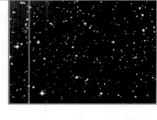

stream a fresh water habitat with moving water *(page B36)* **Plants and animals live in and around a stream.**

Sun the closest star to Earth *(page D7)* **The Sun gives Earth heat and light.**

T

temperature measures how warm something is *(page E9)* **You can find the temperature by using a thermometer.**

V

vibrates moves back and forth *(page E44)* **When air vibrates, you can hear sound.**

volcano a mountain formed when hot, melted rock builds up and bursts through the surface *(page C22)* **Mt. St. Helens is a volcano that erupted in 1980.**

volume the amount of space that a thing takes up *(page E15)* **You can measure the volume of a liquid with measuring cups.**

W

water cycle the movement of water between the ground and sky *(page C8)* **The water cycle creates rain and snow.**

water vapor water that goes into the air *(page C6)* **When water boils, some of the water turns into water vapor.**

woodland forest a habitat that gets enough rain and sunlight for trees to grow well *(page B10)* **Many plants and animals live in a woodland forest.**